Finding Your
Forever Love

Creating and Keeping the Magic in Your Relationship

CONNIE SCHOTTKY- OSTERHOLT

New York

Finding Your Forever Love
Creating and Keeping the Magic In Your Relationship

Cover Design by: Johnson 2 Design   www.Johnson2design.com
Megan@Johnson2Design.com

ISBN 978-1-60037-683-2

Library of Congress Control Number: 2009932818

MORGAN · JAMES
THE ENTREPRENEURIAL PUBLISHER

Morgan James Publishing, LLC
1225 Franklin Ave., STE 325
Garden City, NY 11530-1693
Toll Free 800-485-4943
www.MorganJamesPublishing.com

In an effort to support local communities, raise awareness and funds, Morgan James Publishing donates one percent of all book sales for the life of each book to Habitat for Humanity. Get involved today, visit **www.HelpHabitatForHumanity.org**.

Introduction

As I write this, I am looking at the most stunning view of the Fijian coast. The colors of the sea are magnificent blues and greens and in the distance I can see the waves breaking and their white frosted tops hitting the edge of the reef. My husband of five years, Alexander, is going diving today and I am pondering about what brought me here and how it all happened.

We are here on Fiji to renew our vows and celebrate our fifth anniversary. We met five years and three months ago here in Fiji, fell in love, and returned to Fiji three months later to marry. That sounds too simple, right? It was really simple; we both knew what we wanted and could make the decision to spend the rest of our lives together.

Before we fell in love, I prepared for a long time. I had always thought myself to be a successful woman, except for in one area, the relationship area. After two failed marriages, I decided that I was not good in relationships. I was too independent and too strong to be in a relationship. I decided that I could do without one, I did not need a man. I had great friends, great kids, fantastic work and I would focus on that. So time went by and although my life was really great, I missed being in a relationship. However, little did I realize that I had totally talked myself out of even being able to begin a relationship by saying things like:

- *All the good men are taken*
- *Who would want a 43 year old woman with two kids?*
- *I never meet anyone.*
- *I am pretty special, so I need a special man. I did not meet many people like me, so there must not be many pretty special men around.*
- *I do not want to go into bars and play the dating game.*

I kept myself safe from failing at it again. Not even trying meant also not being hurt or rejected or being afraid it would not work out again. I put on a mask of being totally happy with the situation. Inside though, I was not happy. What I really wanted was to be in a fulfilling relationship. I wanted to come home and find my love there, to share all the joy, all the pleasures as well as the ups and downs of life. I had a great deal of this with my children and my friends, but to have that special somebody just for me, to feel loved and adored, to be taken care of, to cuddle, to cherish and nurture, to have somebody waiting for me, to support, to share intimacy, is what I truly yearned for..

I dreaded trying to figure out how to do this. How was I going to find my love, my soul mate? I didn't know how I was going to do it, but I was at a point where I decided two things:

1) *I was going to be happy, no matter what. Not to be unhappy because I did not have a relationship. Just to be happy. Period!*

2) *I decided to be honest with myself. Dead honest – for the first time in my life I would seriously look at my responsibility in my prior relationships. It is so easy to put the blame on the other person and the circumstances.*

To be happy all the time was actually very easy. The glass is either half full or half empty, you have the choice of how to look at things. You decide how you want to feel. When I looked at my life and saw what I had, two fantastic kids, many wonderful friends, great parents, a career that enabled me to travel and do what I love most, I could not be anything else but happy and when something happened that would make me feel different, I would put a time frame on those feeling and then go back to being happy.

To be really honest with myself was a little more difficult. I had to look at parts of me that were not as attractive as I would have wished them to be. I had to take responsibility for my words, actions and for what was not being said or done. In that moment, I started journaling. I wanted to find out what was working in my prior relationships so I could repeat it. I wanted to know what was not working so I could learn to change this in the future. I was finally ready to look at the lessons my prior relationships provided for me.

I was finally ready to become a student in learning all about myself in relationships. In hindsight, parts of it were really funny and/or stupid, how I thought a relationship would work out all by itself, like magic.

You find a partner, you have those butterflies in your stomach and then you will live happy ever after. Yeah right.

I learned that schools prepare you for a lot in life, but they miss out on teaching you how to create a wonderful relationship. I learned that my selection procedure was non existent. Whoever came by and we had some chemistry going on would do fine for me. I never really looked at what kind of person would be great for me.

I always worried if I was good enough for them .I learned that I never communicated what was really important for me to have, to feel, to do, to be. I learned that I had very specific expectations about how my partner had to act, had to be. Of course I never voiced this and then I was really upset or angry when it did not happen the way I expected it to be. I used to believe that if he really loves me he would know. I learned I wanted everything to be perfect instead of choosing my priorities. I learned about setting boundaries and that I almost never did this. And then when these boundaries were violated I would be so sad, so angry, so hurt that I could not, would not talk about it. I learned so much about me and so much about how I would be and do different the next time. Then I knew it was possible to be successful in a relationship and that even I could make it happen.

After I was married and so obviously happy and radiant, all my friends wanted to know how it happened and especially my single friends wanted to find out in detail what I did. So I looked back in my journal at my notes and I discovered that there was a method to finding my forever love. I had written down everything I did, changed and discovered and acted upon.

I have been talking about it for several years and have coached some of my friends in getting the same results and would like to share my secrets with anyone who wants to learn how to find their own forever love.

It does not matter where you are and what you want, you can make this happen and make yourself happy and fulfilled.

To finding your forever love,

Connie Schottky, Ph.D
Author

Dedication

This book is dedicated to my husband Alexander who is always there for me and supports my every adventure.

Acknowledgements

My heartfelt thanks to my friends Brigitte, Jane, and Doris.

My Anthony Robbins family who witnessed my blooming relationship with Alexander and wanted to know how all of this happened. Especially Deborah Battersby , who made me realize my own limiting beliefs and gave me the resources to cope with my own , imiginairy, challenges.

Mindy who helped me mindmap my thoughts.

And my fabulous friend AnnMcIndoo, my Author's coach, who got this book out of my head into your hands.

Ed Friedel for his editing and critique. And of course my sons Laurens and Pieter for their patience and understanding.

My Mom and Dad

Thank you all.

Preface

This book is written as a result of my own struggles in relationships and how I finally found my way out and then met my fabulous husband. When people asked me how this all happened I looked back at my journal and to my surprise there was an actual method to what I did. This book is written for everybody who wants to have a fulfilling relationship and wants to find or create their own forever love. It is possible, you just have to know how.

Why I am writing this book to give everybody the way to a succesful relationship. The book is a step by step process and will lead you to having a great, wonderful and exciting love.

How this book will help you , just follow the steps and you will be surprised by what happens.

Table of Contents

Chapter One

The Ingredients for a Loving and Passionate Relationship

In this chapter I will discuss the book's goal: helping you, the reader, to find a truly loving and a truly passionate relationship. Here are the ingredients. You should, can and will achieve this!

Mutual Importance is Crucial

In order to make a relationship work, you have to give each other the feeling that you are the most important people in each other's lives. You need to feel that your loved one finds you number one in importance (this is especially true for women), and you need to convey the same to your partner.

There's no one and nothing else more important than that person in your life.

How would it feel if somebody in your life said, "You are number one. I love you so much. And you will always be that important for me." That would feel good, wouldn't it? But the one complaint I hear a lot is: Everything is more important than me—his job, his computer, his sports, his friends. Or: the children come first—after the kids were born, I feel I lost my wife. If you cannot relay the feeling that this specific, this special person is this important, then your relationship will struggle.

The Definition of Important

"Important" means that you each know that you will always come first for your partner. Whatever is going on, you will have the attention of your loved one. You will come first when there is something else going on. There will be time to stop and to listen. Exactly how you are made to feel that you are the most important will be different for everyone. And how you make your partner feel that he or she is the important may be unique. But you each need to express this to your love, and you each need to know your own importance.

When do I feel important in my relationship? I know I am important when I can come up to my husband Alexander at any time no matter what is going on. He stops what he's doing and listens for a moment. We don't always talk at that moment, but we will schedule a time when we can sit down and talk about what's bothering me or what's important for me.

Importance vs. Priority

Priority is something different. Some people confuse importance with priority and say, "In order to be important, to be number one, I need to be with my partner all the time."

Last week, I was talking to a guy who's freshly in love. He was struggling with a conflict. He" knew" intellectually that he had to make his girlfriend the most important thing in his life, but he also felt he had another mission in life. "I have to do something here on earth (he's involved in a very special project.) "That's actually the most important thing in my life—it's my mission."

I told him to hold on, that he was confusing what's important with priorities. In life, we all have priorities. *In a relationship, your partner, your loved one, has to be the most important, but not necessarily the number-one priority all the time.* When you give your girlfriend the feeling that she is most important in your life, then for sure you can do what you want to do in life. You know from each other what to do to give out the special feeling that yes, you are the one, you are my number one, you are the most important in my life. Within this core understanding, you can then establish your own rules. You can each live your mission.

So I have a question for you. What needs to happen for you to feel that you are the most important?

In my relationship, I know for sure that my husband Alexander is most important in my life. If something is going on, I drop everything and travel home to be with him.

But he's not always the number-one priority. I love to do other things in life too! I have a mission in my life. In fact, I have passions for many other things and luckily enough, I have the freedom to pursue them.

The lesson is to make each other number-one in importance, but accept that you're not always number one in priority. So you can each live your lives your own ways, but have the most outstanding, awesome relationship. You can have the freedom to do whatever you want or need to do. You can have it all as long as you both agree on how to set this up, so that both partners feel important AND free to live life to the fullest.

Polarity

There needs to be a polarity in a relationship. Polarity means you like that the other person is different from you, and the difference between the two of you creates that spark, that intimacy, that passion.

A lot of people say, "Polarity? OK—that's just the difference between male and female." That's definitely part of the attraction!

But a relationship needs to have the yin and the yang, the light and the dark, the drive and the energy, the challenge and the praise. The differences between two people create that passion and that intimacy. This is the polarity that you're really looking for.

People have both male and female energy. Where you live at your core will be important in choosing your partner. On the scale from masculine to feminine, there are all possibilities and varieties. When you know where you are, you can find your counterpart. Sometimes you can choose when you want to step into your masculinity or your femininity. Look at what serves the result you want to have. So some choices will be context-related. For example, I choose to be more in my masculine energy when I lead people over the fire in a firewalk, which I do occasionally.

You are most happy, though, when you live most of your time at your core. And in a relationship, you definitely have to choose who is in the masculine energy and who is in feminine energy.

You're not looking for a person that is just like you; that's the ingredient for a great friendship. You look for differences. Again differences create attraction, differences create passion and intimacy.

But you also have make sure that you have some sameness as well. The sameness creates the friendship that you also need in a relationship. If you do not build that friendship, you might get irritated about the differences you were so attracted by in the first place! To see your partner as your best friend as well makes you tolerant and forgiving. I will talk more about this later.

Trust

One of the most important requirements of a good relationship is the ability to trust your partner, your loved one. If there's no trust, there's no real passion and there's no real intimacy. There might be sex, but to create a long-term fulfilling relationship, sex is not enough. So think of what you need in order to develop that trust. What needs to happen for you to trust that person completely?

One of the things that comes to mind is having no ego. When two people have a power struggle, it's about the need to feel significant, it's all about ego. Find your significance in knowing that you have this great love. Find it in knowing that you are the most important person in your partner's life. A man needs to have that trust from his woman in order to feel significant, to feel powerful, to be able to live his purpose.

What's more important in your relationship? Your significance, your ego-- or creating that fulfilling and passionate love?

When you're able to create that trust, and when know that your partner trusts you 100%, you can talk to each other about anything and everything. You each know that you're there for each other all the time when needed. You build up that trust. And it is true trust that builds passionate relationships, because ego has no place in a good relationship.

For sure, you want to feel significant—that's the important part in loving and being loved. But struggle between two partners creates disaster in relationships. Ego? No way! Trust is what you have to go for. What do you need to feel safe with your partner at all times, to feel safe enough to trust completely?

Honesty

Honesty means the ability to tell your partner your true desires and true feelings. What is really important for you? What do you see, hear, and feel? How can your partner give you what you truly want and need? Be honest about what you want and need in a relationship. If you don't say, how does your partner know?

First, of course, you have to be honest with yourself. You know what you want and need in a relationship. Then, you have to have enough courage to tell your partner! We all like to think our partner can mind-read and will magically know what we need to be happy and fulfilled. Well, they don't! I have often heard: If they really love me, they should know what I need. I say, if you know it, you can create it! Tell them exactly what it is that makes you feel sexy. Tell them what it is that makes you feel supported. Tell them what it is that makes you feel happy and fulfilled.

Be honest with yourself, and then find the guts and courage to communicate your findings to your partner. When you tell your partner exactly what makes you happy and fulfilled in your relationship, you will take your relationship to a whole new level. Isn't it worth it?

Before I learned to do this, I never dared to say what was important for me. I thought that was selfish and I did not want to look bad. I was afraid to lose love and respect. Therefore I never totally got what I wanted and needed. And because I did not feel loved and fulfilled the way I needed, I lost love and respect anyway.

Isn't it way easier to just communicate--and to ask in return what makes your partner happy, supported, and fulfilled? We'll talk more about communication below.

Intimacy

Intimacy is that special place where you feel safe and where the two of you are almost like one person, or two people with one life. In my wedding ring, it says, "I am you and you are me." There's a wonderful feeling of oneness, of sometimes not knowing where your body starts and your partner's body ends.

For a woman, without intimacy, there's no enjoyable sex. Without intimacy, there isn't total trust. It's all related. Without trust; no intimacy. Without intimacy; no trust.

In order to create that intimacy, there also needs to be something we call being present. When you're present with your partner, when you're present with your love, you're totally there. So often, we have conversations going on in our head while we pretend to listen. When you're busy with yourself, your inner voice, your thoughts, your action plans for the next day, you're never present. People feel it and sense it.

In order to have true intimacy, you need to be present, you need to be in the moment. When you're in the moment, you can build up that passion and that true intimacy. No wonder the present is a gift. Take time for each other. Take time to really listen to or be silent with each other. Take time to share all of you, without holding back. Take time to acknowledge each other.

Unconditional Love

Unconditional love stems from unconditional acceptance--acceptance first of yourself. Do you accept yourself totally, including all the things you may not want to see—the so-called "bad and the ugly" along with the good and the beautiful? Do you accept yourself unconditionally?

You learn from a young age that love might be conditional. You learn as a small child that when you do things the way your parents or teachers want, when you listen to your mommy and daddy, they love you. But when you're playing with the television remote control, or when you're not doing what you need to do in your potty, then mommy and daddy are not happy with you. So early on, you learn that there is good behavior and bad behavior. And more often than not, you think that it is *you* that is good and bad, and you start liking the good you and disliking the bad you!

You could easily come to the conclusion that you're loved when do the good stuff according to your mom and dad, and that you're not loved when you do the things they don't like.

So we grow up with this concept that love is conditional. There is a certain set of rules for you to follow, and then you'll get love. Although we might have picked that up, that's not the case, because you also know that on another level, your mom and dad love you unconditionally. No matter what you do, they love you.

It might be certain behavior they don't like at that moment. But the real you they love. Similarly, when you accept yourself, when you love yourself, you set yourself up to love and can accept your partner. Separate the behavior from who you really are. Behavior is easily changed when you want to.

Unconditional love is love that separates from, is separate from, everything that's going on. That sounds a bit weird, doesn't it? By separate, I mean you have your love and your put it in a golden box, you tie a beautiful bow around it, and that's your love. It's to be cherished, nurtured. It's sacred.

How do you keep it safe? We don't touch that love. We do not doubt it, we do not insult it nor tarnish it. That love is there to cherish and nurture, to feed with special moments, to feed with even more love. That love is present and it's unconditional.

Whenever there are challenges, things to work out, you do that outside of your love, so you can truly love each other unconditionally. It's such a joy to love with no conditions! Without saying, "When you do this, I love you even more." Decide that every day your love will be stronger and more beautiful than the day before. It should be so unconditional that the love is just there no matter what happens. This has absolutely nothing to do with setting boundaries, which I will talk about later on.

Communication

As I said earlier, communication was for me one of the most difficult things in a relationship. In the beginning, I didn't dare to communicate what I wanted and what I needed because I was afraid when I did that, it would take love away.

Most people think that their partner should be able to read minds. When you are totally in sync with your partner, you'll get the feeling that you "know." Check it, though, to see if you're right. You have a 50-50 chance. When you communicate, do so in a very nice and elegant but passionate way.

People don't know by looking at you what makes you happy. They just act in what they believe is the right way. Most of the time, they treat you as they want to be treated.

I have a great example of this. I have long-time friends. When they were newly married, they were very much in love and had a beautiful home. He thought what would make her happy would be his taking on all the administration—doing the accounts, paying all the bills, taking care of all the correspondence, etc. He thought, "I'll take care of all of this, and we'll live happily ever after." But she wasn't happy during the first couple of months of their marriage. What would have made her happy would have been to get flowers, to get compliments, to get little gifts. He didn't know that.

It was from the goodness of his heart, from his great love for her, that he did all the administrative things he really didn't like. But she was asking herself, "Why is he spending all this time on the accounts, bills, and correspondence? I want him to be with me. I want him to buy me flowers. I want him to buy me little gifts. That would make me happy."

It didn't go well during those first months of marriage, so they got some coaching from a friend. They discovered that the wife actually loved doing all the bills! No problem for her—she really enjoyed it, and in fact, she could do it in much less time than he did. Her husband said, OK, great—you take care of all the administrative stuff, and if the only thing I need to do is bring you flowers and little gifts, I can do this easily. He was very relieved and happy and so was she!

Once they cleared up what they needed to do for each other in order to feel happy, to feel loved, they did these things gladly, and their marriage took off. It's seems like a small thing and it sounds silly to even talk about it, but if you don't know what *really* makes your partner happy or feel loved and supported, you might do the totally wrong thing, and do it out of love.

When you do what feels right for you, but don't know if it's right for your partner, it's hit-or-miss. When we don't know, we automatically go for what makes us happy. Get yourself educated in what your partner wants!

Communication is very important –otherwise, you might have expectations that will never--can never-- be fulfilled, leading to total disappointment. And when you're disappointed in your partner, you go downhill, and that's not what we want, is it? Tell your partner, communicate to your partner what they can do to make you happy, to make you fulfilled, to support you. And of course, ask your partner the same.

What I do with my husband is (we have it all set up already!) is, once in a while I just ask, "Honey, is there something else I can do that makes you feel even more loved? Honey, is there something else I can do that makes you feel even more supported?" Sometimes he says, "No, I'm totally happy, I feel totally supported and loved." Other times, he comes up with a suggestion or something I can do for him. I'd be most happy to do that, and he does the same for me.

Pick the right time to communicate, though. Set up an appointment for it when you both feel great. When you talk, talk about your feelings. How good it will make you feel! Stay with how you want it to be and do not get sucked into how bad it was before. The past is the past—create the future now.

Magical Moments

We all have fond memories of things that have happened in our lives. One of my fondest ones is when I went on holidays with my family. One year we went to Italy in the summer, for the first time to another country. We had such a great time swimming and having fun with the family at the Lido and in the winter we went skiing in Germany. A very small village with just one slope, but for me the place where I learned that I love to ski. I still remember all the places we went to and all the things we did, and I will keep them in my heart forever.

Actually, one of my parents' philosophies was that they'd rather spend all our money and create wonderful family holidays than to save up and have the money sit in a bank. They were so right— because for me those memories last forever.

One of the things that is very important to do in a relationship is to create those special magical moments together. Take time to design a magical moment, whatever you want to do. It doesn't have to be something big like an exotic vacation or an expensive gift—you can create little moments every day.

Here's what my husband did for me one morning when I slept in a little longer. He made me chocolate-covered strawberries. Something simple, but it was a wonderful surprise. Other surprises and special moments might be flowers, love letters, a rose-petal bath, or photos of you and your loved one placed in a very special place so you can remember how happy you were at those moments.

Make it a habit to create at least one special magical moment a day, and then have a plan for creating a couple of big special moments each month or year. Those moments will pull you through when things are not going the right way. Those times are priceless and will add so much to your love.

When you build a foundation of special magical moments, of wonderful memories and things you did together, then you have a solid, sound foundation that will always be there and on which you can build.

It's all about creating that base and that strong connection, so that whenever something happens out of your control that isn't so nice, you have that solid foundation to fall back on.

Another result: When you have that solid foundation, you can take more time out to work, to follow your mission. You know you have the strong connection, and that's the base. That base is built so strongly that it can also withstand the inevitable wear-and-tear of daily life. It can withstand the test of time.

Being a Raving Fan

Being a raving fan means being your partner's number-one supporter.

Whenever I'm travelling from my home country, The Netherlands, to America I love going into a football stadium and seeing people wearing team colors, those scarves, those big foam hands with the "Number One" index fingers! They are the ultimate raving fans. They love their team and their players.

I'd like you to be like that in your relationship. Whatever your partner is doing, support them and tell them how proud you are. Thank them for what they're doing and giving. Be interested in what they're doing and rave about it!

Tell your friends how proud you are of your partner— that they're doing this, or standing up for a cause, or how brilliant they are in their work. Express how wonderful they are with you, your family, your kids, and your friends. Have you ever been with people who speak in a bad or disrespectful way about their partner? Or even indifferently or jokingly call them the old girl, my old man, my ball and chain? How does that make you feel?

So, brag about your partner. Brag about your partner to your partner and to their friends and family. Take on that role of being a raving fan. You cannot rave enough about your partner because in the first place, it makes you feel good, and in the second place, it makes your partner *really* feel good!

Compassion Plus Wisdom is Power
(Buddhist philosophy)

I also have a coaching business. I love helping people sort out their challenges and give them the resources they need. I hear a lot from clients who say, "I don't feel powerful," or "I don't have control in my relationships," or "It's a struggle for who has more power." But power struggles have no place in a relationship. Compassion and wisdom are the ingredients of real power. True power comes from these ingredients.

You need to be compassionate towards your partner and yourself. You need to have the wisdom to know what to do and not do, what to say and not say, what to be and keep and what to let go of. These two elements will give the sense of true power over yourself and true power to make your relationship a really loving and passionate one.

Remember, compassion and wisdom are the two ingredients that will give you the powerful relationship you're looking for. And remember, power is another word for significance. Build up the compassion you have for your partner, be wise in every way for you and your loved one, and then you will truly understand the magic of feeling powerful.

CHAPTER TWO

Getting Real—Being Honest With Yourself

Whether you are currently single or in a relationship here is where you have to ask yourself the tough questions.

What Do You really Want

You're either in a relationship or you're not.

If you're in a relationship, you're either happy with it or you're not. And if you're not, you either want to improve or leave that relationship.

If you're not in a relationship, you have a choice: I want a relationship now, or I'm not in a space right now to find a new relationship. Then I would advise you to give yourself some time to think it over. Decide upon a date by when you will make a decision. It's totally OK wherever you are, but set a timeframe to look at your situation again and decide if you are still happy where you are, or if you want to change your status. You have to be dirt-honest with yourself and set fear and hurt aside.

Say at this moment that you're not in a relationship and you're not particularly interested in having one right now. Fine--but make sure you decide on a date to look at things again in six weeks, three months, six months. Set yourself a specific point in time to re-evaluate.

If you're in a relationship that's not particularly happy at this moment, also set yourself a timeframe. Say to yourself, I'm going to do everything I can to improve my relationship, and I will re-evaluate where I am in three months, six months, a year—it's up to you. But set that timeframe. In my previou marriage I was not particular happy. I gave myself a year to see if things would turn around and I made a commitment to myself to do whatever it would take in this year and after the year I would reevaluate.

For me it did not change around and I know other marriages where it worked fabulously.I do know that it takes two to tango, but I also know that when you change, the reactions you get will change as well. Basically, everything will change because the meaning you give certain things in your relationship will be different, and that energy will change your partner as well. It is the action reaction—different action produces a different reaction.

If you're in a wonderful relationship, congratulations, well-done! But look at what you can do to make it even better, to make sure you keep what you have. Set yourself timeframes to check in periodically where you each are, if you're as happy as you were six months ago (or happier), etc.

The message is: Wherever you are, make sure to set yourself a timeframe. Give yourself dates at which you will re-evaluate where you are. Take time to set up the next game plan.

It's "always" time to get honest with yourself! That's the part I had a hard time with. I didn't want to be honest about my relationships and about myself. It was so much easier to point my finger at my partner and say, it's his fault. He didn't do this, he didn't do that---all those things we all like to say when we're just out of a relationship, because then we're playing the blame game.

You think that it's never your fault. The other person is always to blame, or maybe it's the circumstances. Now is the time to sit down and start being honest. What I did was to get out my journal and start writing about my role and what my responsibility was in all of my prior relationships.

I wrote about how I co-created what happened, or how I allowed it to develop by not communicating (or communicating in the wrong way), or by the decisions I made (or did not make).

Learn the Lessons in Your Relationship

There are lessons in your relationship. I never wanted to accept that. I only said to myself, I'm successful in many areas in my life, but I'm not successful in relationships. But I had no clue that there were important lessons to be learned from them.

When you don't learn the lessons, they will confront or defeat you again and again until you finally are ready to admit that you obviously had to learn something! In my case, I had to learn a lot.

Once I was ready to accept that there were lessons for me to learn from my past relationships, then I started to journal. I started to see what worked and what didn't work. I started to see clearly what it was that I needed and wanted in a relationship. I had never looked at myself that way before. I had always asked what I could add, what I could bring, to the relationship. But when you aren't certain what it is that you need, how can you find or create it?

What Worked and What Did Not?

To learn the lessons in your relationships, you first have to look at what really worked in them.

And at first, I didn't want to try to look at what was good because I thought it was all horrible. Maybe you're the same. But be honest again. Go and take another look at your relationships because there were definitely parts that were good. There were parts of them that you loved. There were times where you had fun. There were aspects that you felt good about. So get your journal out and start writing down what worked in your relationships, the past ones and when you are in a relationship right now, your current one as well. Things are never all bad. Go look for what clicked so that you can remember them in your next relationship.

- Why did you fall in love with this person?
- What was good about your relationship?
- Where did you have fun in your relationship?
- What parts did you really like about that specific relationship?

Now you will understand yourself better as well. You will have a better feeling about the time you were with this partner.

Once you've done this, then do exactly the same for what did not work—write them down. It may be that you are no longer in a relationship, but you might think that it was the most amazing relationship ever. But there must have been parts that didn't work so well, parts that were missing. Write down all the things that you did not have in that relationship, or that did not work for you.

- What did not/ does not work in your relationship?
- What were/are you irritated about?
- What did/do you dislike?
- What was/is unacceptable?

Think about what you've written down to learn more about yourself.

What Was/Is Your Responsibility?

After you've written all of this down--what worked and what didn't—then look at how you created these outcomes. When it comes to what didn't work, believe me, I know that these are not the nicest things to look at. My point is that you did have a responsibility then, and you have a responsibility now, to look back, learn, and use the past to help you in the future.

In The Netherlands we say that when two people are fighting, two people are guilty—one for starting the fight and the other one for allowing it or continuing it!

So, yes, although you've recorded all the things about your partner and your time with him or her that weren't so good, you also have to look at *your* part in creating or continuing these negative parts of your relationship:

- What part were/are you responsible for?
- What were/are the things that you did knowing they weren't right to do?
- What were/are the things you should have done, but didn't?
- What were/are the things you said in that relationship that weren't the right things to say?
- What were/are all the things you didn't say in that relationship, although you knew you should have spoken up?
- What were/are the boundaries you set, the rules you had in your relationship-- or boundaries you didn't set, rules didn't you communicate?

Take responsibility for the fact that that relationship didn't work out. When you get past the fact that "the relationship didn't work out" and instead dig in and look at what you yourself created, what part you were responsible for, this is where you will learn the most important lesson.

What References Do You Have From Your Friends and Family?

You have to be very careful whom you hang out with. Hopefully, they all love you, but some people do and say things that aren't helping you. I know back then, when I was in my late twenties, my family said, when my first marriage didn't work, that I had a good life, that I was very successful, but maybe this was just the one area I would not be good at. They said I should accept this. Friends and family said that I was too critical, that I could never have it all, that I had to compromise.

When I was a little older, they said, what do you want? You're 45, you have two children, and men are not waiting in line for a wife with two kids—so accept it. The message I got from friends and family was to accept my situation and be happy with it.

That's not a good message to get. Be careful what you take in and what you start to believe. You know they mean well, but you don't have to adopt these or any other references. They're theirs and that's fine. Leave them with them—they don't have to be yours.

Take a look at what your friends say about you and your relationship. Look at what your family says about you and your relationship (or about your not being in one). Look at what they believe about you, about your circumstances, and about your actions and needs in regard to relationships.

Write it all down, take a look. Determine if their beliefs and advice are helping you get to where you really want to be, or if they're actually stopping you from reaching your desired goal.

People say there are more women than men in the world, so why do you expect that all women will have a relationship? They also have beliefs about age--that once you're over a certain age, then it's almost impossible to hook up. They have beliefs about age differences in relationships. They have beliefs about the roles of different religions and cultures in the context of forming successful relationships.

So I'm encouraging you to really look at what they have to say. Then, either keep their beliefs or give them back! The choice is yours.

What Do You Focus On?

What do you focus on? Do you focus on some of these things you hear from your friends and family? On cultural and global references (which may be reflected in what you hear from your family)? Are you focusing on your hurt from past relationships (so much so that maybe you don't want one anymore, and you will do anything to avoid ever getting hurt again)? Are you focusing on your being alone? When you focus on solitude, you create solitude.

Did you ever decide to buy a new car? Previously you had never noticed a certain model, but now that you've made the decision to purchase one, all of a sudden you see it everywhere. That's what focus is about. What you focus on, you will create.

When you focus on something, then that will be what you see, what you create, and what you attract into your life. When you focus on hurt, when you focus on being alone, then that's what you create and attract.

When you focus on, "I hate being so vulnerable in a relationship," then you hate being vulnerable. And if you focus on, "Hey, I'm over 40 and it's not easy for someone over 40 to find a partner," then you focus on your age as a factor. When you create that, a lot of people will also think that, and also say, "OK, he or she is over 40—it won't be easy." You will find yourself in a group of friends and acquaintances who think the same way. That may be comforting, but it doesn't get you what you really want. So be very careful about what you focus on right now, and what you focus on from the past.

Excuses

Take a real good and hard look at what excuses you use to NOT get what you want. What do you tell yourself? What story do you like to tell yourself and others and hang onto for dear life in order to not do or not get what you want? Write down what excuses you use.

I had a lot of excuses not be in a relationship. When my second marriage did not work out and I was mid forty I said that I had been there, done that. That I was special and needed a very special man. That there weren't many of me, so there weren't going to be many special men around. That I never met anybody. I was actually in an environment where I met literally thousands of new people every year, yet I still had the same stories, the same excuses—so I never "met" anybody new. What you tell yourself is what you create.

I told myself that I didn't need a man, that I could do it all myself. That I didn't miss being in a relationship, that it was great to be by myself. That I had all the freedom that I had never had when I was involved with somebody else.

I have a friend who tells herself that her body would need to be in perfect shape and that she would need to be financially independent before she could attract a partner. Another friend always says, "I don't have time right now—later, when I'm not so busy with my business." Yet another friend says, "I only ever meet married men!"

What do you say to yourself? What excuses do you have? What stories do you have? Write them down, because when you write them down, you can really look at them, and hopefully, you will laugh out loud when you see them!

What Would Happen If You Knew For Sure You Would Find the Right One?

Think for a moment. What would happen if you KNEW you would be totally successful? If you just KNEW you could find the right partner, you just KNEW that you would find this great relationship?

You would do everything and anything because you would be sure it was out there for you.

I don't work in network marketing, but there is this great example I picked up from this field. In network marketing, they get a lot of people who say "no" to the product or the business opportunity. They say you have to work through your no's to get to your yesses. Their example is: If you have a bucketful of oysters, and in that bucket there are two oysters with the most magnificent pearls you will ever see, are you going to go and open every single oyster? Of course you will, because you know there's a big reward. You know that those beautiful pearls are waiting for you. You know you cannot fail— it's certain that those two pearls are there.

If you know for sure that the right relationship is waiting for you. "If you know for sure that there is that one person that's especially for you. If you know for sure that you can make a success out of your relationship. If you know for sure that you can have a wonderful, loving, caring, and beautiful relationship, aren't you going to do whatever it takes to get there? Aren't you going to search through all the oysters? Won't you have a different attitude? Won't you have a different feeling about it? So start building up this certainty, this faith. My belief is that there is somebody out there for everyone.

Committed or Interested?

I think most people are interested in having a great relationship, a wonderful partnership. I really do. But then, there a difference between being interested—it would be nice if you had it—and being committed. Being committed means doing whatever it takes.

Vince Lombardi, the great football coach, once said, "In order to be successful, what you need to do is anything and everything."

So in order to be successful in your relationship, be committed enough to do whatever it takes. Don't go, "I dated ten people over the last five years, and things didn't work out." Do you do a lot, or do you sit down and wait until things happen for you? Are you the one who goes there and says, "You know what, I'm just going to do whatever it takes, because I know this great relationship is waiting for me."

When you're committed, you will create that. When you're committed, you will do whatever it takes. You will go out and play that oyster game. If one oyster doesn't have the pearl, the next might have. You just go on until you find that beautiful pearl, *confident that you will find it.*

Create a Happy Life

This is the one decision I made that I remember so clearly. At a certain point, after none of my relationships had worked out, I was in the middle of processing everything and learning about myself, learning about having and taking responsibility for these outcomes.

Then, all of a sudden, I decided to be happy, no matter what! I know the exact time. I know where I was. I know what I was doing. I was teaching and helping out at a training for coaches and I was sitting in the back of the room, I had a quiet moment and it dawned on me that I was living the life I always wanted. I was travelling the world, teaching, coaching, speaking. I had great friends, awesome children. I had every reason in the world to be happy. And up till then I connected my happiness to whether I was in a good relationship or not. I decided to be happy at the spot. Simply be happy and do not wait for someone to make me happy. I would make me happy. I am in control of my happiness, what a relief it was for me. It was all of a sudden so easy, so joyful.

When you decide to be happy no matter what's going on in your life, you feel good about yourself. You will look at your life and you will say, "My life and what I have are wonderful. What I'm doing is wonderful. I have wonderful friends in my life." Whether you're in a relationship or not, it doesn't matter—you have decided that from now on, you will be happy.

When you create a life of happiness, your self-esteem goes up and your confidence will shine through. As a result, you will be attractive-- people will want to be around you. People want to be around happy people. People will want to be in *your* company.

When you are at that stage, you will attract people into your life. The chances that you will attract "the one" you want to be with, your loved one, is practically 100%.

Start smiling at everybody you meet. Write down what you already have in your life that makes you happy--- everything, big and small. Count your blessings—all of them. You will soon see that you have many that you had taken for granted or failed to see or acknowledge. Start practicing the art of being happy with who you are and where you are in your life. If you want to improve something, go right ahead—make a plan, and take all the action you need step-by-step. But be happy now! Don't wait until everything is "perfect." The right time to be happy is NOW!

CHAPTER THREE

The Consequences of Bad Experiences

In life there are always consequences we might not think about upfront.

Negative Thoughts

What are your negative thoughts? Some of mine were, "All the good guys are married or taken" or "I'm not perfect—before I get into a relationship I should wait until I've sorted out all my stuff or I've bought my own house." When you think like that, you can wait forever and never have the courage to find the partner who's right for you.

I have a dear friend who seriously asks the question, "Why do all relationships end after three months?" She has the idea in her brain that every one lasts for only this period. Again, if you focus on that, guess what? That's what going to happen.

We are so critical of ourselves. "I need to go work out—my muscles aren't developed enough." "I'm too fat." "I'm too old."

The list is endless. I have kids—and I can't go into a relationship with kids! What would happen if my new partner didn't like kids? But the kids are my everything—they are the most important thing in my life. And what would happen if they didn't like my new partner? Stepmother, stepfather...this never works out. There is always a struggle. . .

When you have these thoughts, do they keep you from even trying to find somebody? You ask yourself questions such as, "Where do I find them?" and give yourself the negative answer, "I will never meet them." How about, "I'm not the marrying kind. I want my own space. The last thing I would want is to live together."

Or you may think, "I'm a career man, I'm a career woman—that's really important for me, and none of my relationships so far could understand that." Or "I have my own house, it's very nice, and I feel great in it. If all of a sudden, another person moved in, they'd move everything around and I'd have to empty my cupboard space. I just arranged everything the way I want it."

When you think like that, you stop yourself from even looking for a relationship. you think of everything that can go wrong. You think of everything you'd have to *give up* instead of thinking what you will *gain*.

Replaying Dating Experiences

Most people who have been in relationships give up on the thought of dating and say, "I dated forever. I don't know how to meet any more people." Internet dating? "I don't want to go on the Internet today. There are only creeps out there who put up false profiles in order to get you into bed. You never know how to select anyone because no one is telling the truth."

Replaying all those bad experiences isn't going to bring you where you want to be. Don't let bad old memories stop you from looking for your new special someone.

Get some new references. Have you ever sat on a terrace or at a café and just watched people? I love France. There are a lot of terraces and cafés, and one of things I enjoy is sitting at them just looking at people. Have you ever seen couples that you never would have put together? Have you seen an ugly man with a stunning woman and thought, "How on earth did *that* happen?" It could be the other way around—an attractive, handsome man with kind of a mousey, plain, homely woman. What did she do? How did *she* attract *him*?

Do a reality check, and look at your own negative thoughts. If you let your experiences from the past stop you from dating and finding that beautiful love that's in store for you, please think again.

Perhaps you say to yourself, "It's not meant to be. Why even bother? I can save myself the energy. I can save myself from going through all of those people again. I'm fine on my own. It's way too much effort. I've been there, I've done that."

That's what's stopping you! Write down all the thoughts you have that came from the references and experiences you had dating in the past.

The good thing about the past is—it's over. You don't have to bring it into the present—you're done with it. Don't let it stop you creating what you want to be and have.

Out of those bad experiences, we've built up a lot of negative beliefs. We believe, for instance, that men are bastards, they're selfish and superficial, they only want somebody who looks good, is six feet tall and slim—that's the only thing they're interested in.

Or—men are holding you back, they put you down, they want you at the stove cooking for them and at the sink cleaning up for them. They don't understand you.

When you have all these negative beliefs about men, what would happen if you actually met a nice guy? Would you project all those beliefs onto him? Probably. Would that then work out? Probably not.

It's the same for men. Men believe women are needy, clingy, expensive—high-maintenance in every sense and that when you're in a relationship, you lose freedom. So if you think these ways about women and you meet this really nice beauty, what do you project onto her? You project all the negatives, despite any realities. It's all in your mind, but you're looking for it, and so you'll find it!

Dating is just a numbers game. Remember the oysters. Make dating fun. Go out with at least three people at the same time! Dating is just to find out if you want to go out again until you are certain that this person is the one you've been looking for. Then you can mutually commit to being exclusive. Keep it light, keep it fun, and, most important, don't let the past discourage you. We'll talk more about this in a later chapter.

Consequences of Being Hurt

Sometimes you might have been truly and badly hurt by a previous relationship. You may still feel intense hurt and sadness. If there's always a chance that another one would end the same way, why would you try it again?

If you predict that the outcome of a relationship will be that your partner will eventually leave you and/or hurt you, well, that's a good reason you would never want to try again. Your thinking is a big consequence of your bad experience. Thinking this way might certainly leave you gun-shy and holding back. It would leave a lot of people unwilling to make any future commitment. That is why it is so important for you to remember the good times as well!

People who don't want to make a commitment because they've been hurt in the past are actually clinging to that hurt. They do whatever they can to protect themselves. When you're in that position, then you're emotionally unavailable for a new relationship until you clear that space. You can clear that space by doing some soul-searching. Go to a personal development course, get a coach, journal. Staying home or hanging out with your friends, are not taking real actions. Remember that living in the same space every day may be comfortable, but it won't be fulfilling.

I have this beautiful girlfriend. She's pretty, with blond hair and brown eyes, but she has been hurt in past relationships. What she does is stay on the safe side. Yes, she does go out, but she goes out with a group of girlfriends, and she only connects with her group of girlfriends. Even though she's out there, the only people she interacts with are her girlfriends, because it's safe.

People who cling to their hurt most likely postpone things. They say, "I would love to have a relationship, but not today, not this month, not this year—maybe next year." Maybe never—they continue to postpone. In some way their past hurt is protecting them from possible hurt in the future, but at the same time it is preventing them from possible love and bliss, fulfillment, and passion. They are still focusing on the negative things that might happen, and forgetting about all the beautiful things that might open up.

They may pretend not to care, but they totally close up when meeting someone new. They may meet someone very suitable, but they don't open up because their negative experiences from the past prevent them from seeing what a beautiful person they have right in front of them. They don't see how beautiful life and love can be when we give them a chance!

The Questions You Ask Yourself

You constantly ask yourself questions, even if you don't realize it. There is always an inner dialogue going on, as if there were another person living in your head, and the questions usually start with "Why. . .?"

When you ask a "why" question, there's usually not a good answer. When you ask yourself a "why" question, your brain goes, "I don't know," and when you hear this answer, you go into doubt.

The questions that people usually ask themselves in regard to relationships usually revolve around the larger question, "Why don't they see my good qualities?"

- Why don't they see who I really am?
- Why don't they see the beauty inside of me?
- Why don't they see all the love in me?
- Why don't they see I'm such a caring person?
- Why do they always break up with me?
- Why am I not good enough?

or similar ones.

If you have these questions running through your mind, write them down. Maybe they're on a subconscious level, and you'll have to dig down a little. Ask yourself: Is there anything I ask myself on a consistent basis?

What is going on here? Start writing down the questions you ask yourself. If you know your questions, you can turn them around into other questions that will help you. You will not get that helpless feeling that you're not in control, and that it is always other people's fault. No—take control! Ask yourself, "*How* can I. . ." Start all the questions with a "How. . ." and reword them. For instance; how can I show the real me? How can I express even more of who I am? How can I show people my loving and caring side?

Statements You Make About Blame

A lot of people I've spoken to refuse to look at themselves or their actions at all. They point the finger and say, "But it's their fault, they're wrong, they're to blame," or they blame the circumstances.

I was once talking to a man, not about relationships. He had been fired from different jobs three times in a row, and instead of looking at what he could have done differently, he only said, "My boss didn't understand me. My boss didn't see how good I was." He blamed his bosses.

He also blamed circumstances: "The job was too crazy. The job was too demanding. I had to travel too far and too frequently. The team did not like me."

When you're looking at a situation, and it's *always* the fault of other people, the circumstances, the friend that advised you wrongly, the mother that wasn't nice—then you have to do a reality check. You have to check in by asking what was the part YOU played?

In your partnerships, what were *you* responsible for? Again, be honest --it's never ever only "their" fault. So, again, look at what you're going to do, say, believe, or focus on differently. If you do the same things over and over, you will end up with more of the same results. If you haven't been able to achieve a lasting, happy, loving relationship, maybe you could do a few things differently. What are they?

What Actions?

What can you do now? What actions can you take? What are you doing now? Do you have a social life? Do you go out, to functions, to concerts? Or do you stay home?

If you want to have a relationship yet you never go out, you make it hard on yourself. Sometimes he's knocking on your door, but the chances of that are very small. So what actions have you taken lately?

Be honest. Look at the clothes you wear. Maybe sometimes you just slip into anything comfortable, perhaps a little too comfortable, which may not look good or attractive on you. Especially in your free time, do you wear old scruffy stuff? Or, at the other extreme, when you're out, do you wear only your power or business suits?

What are you thinking about? What do you say to yourself? Sometimes inside your head there is a sort of mantra going on—you may say things over and over, sometimes on a subconscious level. Look at the things you have a habit of saying.

Forgiveness

You have probably had bad experiences, and you know what? Most everybody else has too! I think 99% of us have had negative or downright bad experiences in our relationships.

Just think about the time when you were first in love. Think of your first "real" partner. Wasn't it beautiful? Didn't you totally treasure it? But did it work out? For most people, unfortunately the answer is no.

Let's talk about forgiveness again. Maybe you can't forgive yourself for being in those relationships. Maybe you can't forgive your partners, or others involved in those relationships.

Maybe you can't forgive yourself or others for being fallible, for being human.

So start counting . . .

- How many relationships have you been in?
- How many people did you not forgive, including yourself?
- How many people do you bring with you into a new relationship?

Maybe you bring all the heaviness of that guilt, that hurt, or that sadness into a new relationship. Do you really want to start that way? Forgive that person! You may not be able to forget , but you can forgive . Let go of the pain. Go to the ocean and let the tide take it out. Give it to a tree and bury it underneath. Write it down and flush it down the toilet. Or burn it! Let it go. Who wants to live in the past? It's gone. Live now!

You can use whatever happened in your old relationships to set new boundaries. We'll talk about that, but now it's most important to forgive yourself for making those choices. Forgive those others for making their choices at that time. They didn't know any better. You have the choice of either beating yourself up for the choices you made or saying, at that time I didn't know any better. Those were my choices back then. I've grown since. Now I will make and take other choices.

If you're not able to forgive yourself, you're judging yourself and you're judging other people. I don't know about you, but I don't like to be judged.

We come back to what I talked about earlier about unconditional acceptance. From unconditional acceptance comes unconditional love. Start forgiving. Start accepting yourself for everything you did and every choice you made. Start saying to yourself, "I love you anyway." Accept yourself in the fullest sense.

Would I make different choices right now? Yes, of course I would. But time has gone by. I'm older, I'm wiser, and I've learned from my past. And now I'm able to make better choices for myself.

CHAPTER FOUR

What Do You Really Want and Need in a Relationship?

It's often easy to set goals for different areas in our lives, but we frequently forget to set relationship goals, and That's what this chapter will be about

Decide What You Really Want

Are you like the many people who set goals once a year — on their birthday or around New Year's Eve? That's great — fantastic. I do have some questions for you, though.

- What do you actually do with your goals after you've written them down?
- Are you just happy having them down on a piece of paper, and then you hope that miraculously you will achieve them? And then do you wait and not look at them until the next year?

Let's start with the last point. From my own experience—and also from seeing how my friends set their goals—more often than not, the goals we set are for just two or three areas our lives. Some people are good at setting goals for their career. They might also set goals for their finances or for their health. But very rarely do you see people setting goals for the relationship area. I was one of the vast majority who didn't.

I never thought of making a plan for my relationship, but I probably should have. I never did that, till I came to the realisation that I had to be real clear about what I wanted. It's not as tangible or specific as, for instance, setting money or career goals. So people think it will be more difficult. Actually it is very easy to do so.

So how do you set goals in these areas? The fact is, when you don't know exactly what you want to have, you won't know where to go or how to achieve it. *It's very important to know precisely what you want in a relationship.*

We have a game in Holland. You draw a big picture of a donkey. It's called "Pin the Tail on the Donkey." You're blindfolded and try to pin the tail in the right place. But you might end up somewhere totally different! It can be just like in the world of relationships.

Seeing your goal clearly will help get you there; otherwise, it's pure luck. Some people do have that luck, but it's rare. *You're better off making a clear plan about everything you need and want, and then working your way towards it, step by step.* In earlier times, it was very clear what the roles in a marriage or other relationship were. Men brought in the money (or, earlier, men hunted and brought home the food), and women took care of the kids and the household.

There were a lot of marriages and other partnerships built on such economic benefits, but those times are long gone. Women can now choose freely whether to take care of the children and the household or have a career, or do both. (And of course, men now also have the same choices.) Women have choices equal to men. Women can bring in their own money and be quite independent. But in order to be fulfilled and happy, we women still want a relationship.

In earlier days, women were attracted to men who could literally bring home the bacon, who could provide for and protect the family. Women can now do these things themselves—so, now what?

Most of us can also do impeccable housekeeping, and make sure the laundry is done perfectly. We can look after our children, or hire somebody to do that for us. We can do all this by ourselves, so now what would you need, what would be your choice? Sometimes life looks easier when there are more limited choices. But following the old cultural rules and the old set of limited choices will not make most of us happy and fulfilled.

It's very important to sit down and really determine what you want—actually, not only what you want, but what you need in a relationship. When you get what you want and what you need, you fill yourself up and from that place, you can give out endlessly.

You have to start with *what is important for you in general* to determine what you need in a relationship.

- What makes you happy?
- What qualities do you need in your partner?
- What are the conditions that you need to have in place in order for you to feel great and wonderful in your relationship?

Let's talk about the first point. In order to know *what makes you happy*, you have to look at every area in your life. What do you want as far as health, money, career, emotional life, spirituality, looks, habits, friends, family, hobbies, ways of communicating, sexuality, and so on? It's not enough to only look at the relationship area. You have to look at every area of your life, so you can see the whole package.

Now, let's take the second point. What qualities do you need in your partner? Are looks important to you? Is it important for you that they have personal hygiene, that they're clean? Is it very important that they work out? Is it important what they eat? What are your preferences?

What kind of hobbies do you have? What kind of hobbies would be attractive in a partner? If you have a partner whose hobby is going to a bar or café and watching football games, and you hate football, then that is setting yourself up for a lot of dissatisfaction. But if one of your hobbies is football and your partner is really into it, then you make it easy for yourself.

If you like to go to the Amazon and do trekking in the wild and your partner likes to go to luxury resorts, then you're in for a challenge again. The trick is to find commonality—so set things up from the start to make things easy for yourself.

What kind of career would you want your partner to have? Again, what are your own interests? If you totally don't like computers and your partner is into them, you may have a problem.

What about money? Money is one of the things that creates the most upset in relationships. Money is the one thing you need to speak about early. What if you're into making money, you love making money, and you're created abundance for yourself—and you end up with a partner who thinks money isn't important. Or maybe money is something he or she despises. What if you your partner doesn't want to work or take financial responsibility? You have to first really think about what you want in this all-important area, and then talk about it!

Think about money. What's important for you in this area? It's important for you to understand that up front and then reach an understanding with a partner.

What kind of lifestyle do you want to have? When I created my list that resulted in meeting my current wonderful husband Alexander, I didn't want to have a partner who had a 9-to-5 job. I'm traveling all the time and I can go whenever I want because I create my work around it. I needed to have a partner who could travel frequently, or who at least liked to travel.

It's very important for you to think about your current lifestyle, and what your partner would have to be or have in order for you share that same life. Someone who hates traveling wouldn't be a good match for me.

Next, take a look at family and friends. I know people who love having an extended family. They adore having that extra family. They also would love to have hundreds of friends. But I also know people who like to be more by themselves, who have a very small circle of friends. What's your attitude towards family and friends? I would love to have a family where I'm welcome and to which I feel a connection. I would want my partner to have friends who welcome me, who are open and have similar interests.

How about manners? What kind of manners do you want your partner to have? I'm very picky about how people eat, but that's just me. I was raised very-proper-European, so we eat with a knife and fork and sit up straight and all that stuff. I was with a guy back then that ate with his nose in his plate, and I didn't care for that. It wasn't a small thing for me. You have to determine what would be acceptable to you.

Another example: I like my husband to open the door for me. It's just something I like. I have a friend who totally dislikes it when a partner opens the door for her. It makes her feel small, weak. What's important for you? For me, to be with somebody who doesn't care about manners, or has manners that are totally different from mine, would be a stretch and a challenge. You have to know what's important for you in this area.

How about spirituality? Here is an area that has different meanings for different people. Some think that spirituality means organized religion and a specific religious denomination. Some people might say, time for yourself, meditation. But if you end up with a partner who has a totally different idea of spirituality, that can be a challenge for you.

Make sure you know what spirituality means for you. Make sure you find somebody with similar attitudes.

I'm not specifically into a particular church, but I'm very religious. And I want my partner to have similar beliefs about God and religion. I love to meditate. I love to go to personal development seminars and read personal development books. Make sure that you define what spirituality means to you, so you can attract somebody who is in that same space.

Next you have to look at emotions. Traditionally, women have been allowed to display emotion, whereas men have not been. Nowadays that's also changed. Most men learn that it's great to show emotion and it's great to be able to tap into feminine energy. We both have the male and the female energy in us. I personally like a man who can tap into his feminine energy, who can be sensitive, who can talk to me openly. I like a man who's not afraid to show his emotions.

I wouldn't like it if he lived in that feminine space all the time—that's not what I want. However, I still want a partner who can access that part of himself. That's wonderful for me.

Make sure whether you want to have a partner who is really emotional. If that's what you want, understand that you're going to get the good, the bad, and the ugly!

I wanted to have a partner that I could express myself freely to. I wanted to have a partner that wasn't scared when I expressed all my emotions, when I was other than totally happy, when I sometimes cried. So that is what I put on my list.

It sounds silly, but yes. food. I like vegetables, I like fish. So if I were to have a partner who ate meat all the time, that wouldn't work very well for me. If you love meat, great; but if you have a partner who never eats meat or who has a "thing" about eating it, that wouldn't be a good fit for you. So food is also something you have to think about.

The next area is personal development. Are you into growing? Are you into having a lot of interests? Are you willing to change some things in yourself? Are you willing to look at and learn new things, go to seminars, and meet new people? It would be great if your partner had those interests as well.

Personal development is an area that is very important to me and to which I devote a lot of time. That has to be okay with my partner. So look at what your needs are in this area, and then visualize how you'd like your partner to be.

Next, look at character traits. What character traits do you want your partner to have? For me, it's important that my partner be honest. Honesty is a must for me. I cannot live with somebody who is not honest. Integrity is also very important. I need to be able to believe that when my partner says or promises something, then it will be done.

Make your own list and be sure that you write down what are the most important character traits for you. Knowing what you want in this key area in the key person in your life will help you get it; from there, you can develop the trust that leads to intimacy and passion.

Children

If you don't have any children, and you're not in a relationship, you need to ask yourself if you want kids. If your eventual partner wants kids and you don't (or vice-versa), there's possible trouble ahead.

I have two kids, two wonderful children, so I needed my partner to be somebody who loved children. Also, since I was sure I would not have any more children, I needed my partner to be happy with my two and not want to have another little one.

Guess what—I created that. I attracted the most wonderful husband, who adores my two children, and say things like, "I'm so happy that I just missed the diaper period because that's something I wouldn't have looked forward to."

It's very important to agree about the subject of children. If you don't, then your relationship will probably have a short life—you'll make each other miserable. Again, it's not good, it's not bad—it's just what you and your partner want.

If you both want children, it's also critical that you agree on how you want to raise them. What values will be important to give to your children? What rules, what standards, will you have in the house?

How Do You Want Your Partner to Talk About You?

This is very important to me, and I'm very specific in my wishes here. I like to feel, in a way, significant when he introduces me or talks about me. I love when he uses nice and caring word s. It makes me feel good. What about you? Remember I talked about being a raving fan for each other?

You've all heard the expressions, "Here's my old lady," or "Here's my old man." I don't like them. I don't want to be referred to like that. Spouses even refer to their partners in their 20's in this way—it has nothing to do with age.

I want my partner to introduce me, for example, with "This is the love of my life," or this is the woman I adore, this is the person I love spending my love with, or this is my best friend in the whole wide world. Write down how you would want to be introduced by your partner. By the way, I can't stand a person who forgets to introduce their partner, so set up the rules for this up front as well!

And how would you want to be talked about? I like my partner to rave about me, to be proud of me, to tell people what's great about me, what great things I'm doing—and not to say she's traveling again, she's left me alone again. So, very specifically, how do you want your partner to talk about you? I call my husband Alexander, my love, hon. And, I tell him frequently how proud I am of him. I thank him for what he does for me.

Keeping It Romantic

Do you want to spend a lot of time together, or just a limited amount of time? Do you only want to see each other on the weekends? What kinds of things do you want to do together? Hang out, watch a movie at home, go out to a movie?

What would make you feel there is a romance going on? Do you want to have cards or flowers sent to you? Surprise gifts? Set things up so you feel wonderful and you feel like you're being courted. What do you really want on the romantic side? You can design it right now.

Time

How much time do you want to spend together? Think about it. I see couples who work together the whole day, say eight hours; then afterwards, they go home and they say, "We've spent so much time together already, now I'm going to do my own thing." Is that something you'd want?

For me, it's important when we work the whole day that after we come home we have time to spend an hour together just to catch each other up. We can decide to just sit together and cuddle, or sit together and read a book, or sit together and have a talk—but that hour together, when we really create that quality time together, is very important for me.

We both work very hard—and that's great because we love it—but we need to have at least one day a week where we can do something together. So design some time for yourselves. How much time is important for you—daily, weekly, or monthly—to spend together?

I love going on holidays. In fact, I don't think I've met anybody who doesn't love going on holiday. But how many holidays and when? We love short holidays. Once a month, we love going someplace for a couple of days. It's important that you establish how much time you want to spend with your loved one, and how you spend it.

Values

What do you value most in life? It would be great if you conveyed that to each other. It would be even greater to share your top four with your partner. Your values do not have to be in the exact same order, but they need to "be there." What values are most important to you? Discuss things like family, love, health, growth, honesty, and so on.

If you have, for instance, health in your top four or five, it's great if your partner has it there too. If love is valued as your number one or two, how wonderful if your partner is in sync. If your values are totally different from each other's, then, again, things will be difficult.

If one of your highest values is your need for certainty and one of your partner's is adventure or freedom, then you will have a challenge. It's not that you cannot work out a challenge, but if you know it up front, then you can set things up so you both are satisfied.

Age

What age do you want your partner to be? It's funny, because I made my own list the way I talked with you right now, and the one thing I didn't look at was age.

When I met Alexander, it was immediately clear that he was younger than I. At first, I was concerned because there are all these universal beliefs about age, one of which is that the man should be older than the woman. Because of his age, at first I told him, "You're nice, I like you, but you're way too young for me. I can't do this. Luckily, Alexander did not give up on me. I might have missed out on my biggest chance, the biggest love of my life. That is 7 years ago and they have been the happiest ever.

I suggest that you determine what age range you'd want to partner to have. Would it be okay if he or she were five or ten years older or younger? Give yourself a realistic range.

Say that you're okay with your partner being ten years older—you still have to make sure that your energy levels match. Age also ties into energy. As we get older, our energy decreases. If you're one of those energetic men or women out there, then you need to have an energetic partner. Remember, age can also be mind over matter. If you don't mind, it doesn't matter! So make sure you're comfortable with not only your age range, but with your respective energy levels.

Sometimes with a big age difference, you're at different stages of life. What stage of life are you in? How about your partner? Do you want to retire or go out and explore the world? When we get older, most of us settle down and don't want to travel so much, sometimes not at all—and often that's what you see. It doesn't have to be this way. It isn't necessarily related to age—but it's definitely related to the energy level at which you want to live. Take a look at the pace and the lifestyle you want to have, and determine if your prospective partner would be compatible.

Sex

What about sex? It's a very important part of a relationship. It may not be the most important part, but it's definitely a very enjoyable part, so what about it?

Take a look at how you want that part of your life to be. Are you very adventurous in that area or very conservative? What's most important for you here? It's important to think about this because there can be challenges if you don't. You need to know your boundaries—what you like, what you don't like, what you think is acceptable and what not. What do you want to have or not have? Understand this clearly, and then you can share and communicate this with your partner.

I hear people say, "I want to have more sex. My partner only wants it once a month, but I could do it every day." You need to discuss this and make sure that you get your needs met in this area. And remember, there are all forms of sex. Some you might like and some you might not. Be open-minded here. Take a look and see what could be enjoyable and meaningful for both you and your partner.

Intimacy

As we saw in Chapter 1, intimacy is something different from sex. Yes, with sex, you're very intimate, but it's a physical intimacy. You also need emotional intimacy. So what's important to have there?

Traditionally, men have more interest in sex than intimacy, and women love intimacy sometimes even more than sex. This is "traditionally": what is it that *you* want?

Intimacy means the moments you share with your partner where you feel so close, where you feel so cared for, where you feel so loved and supported. That's true intimacy.

It is so important to feel connected at the deepest levels. It's important to know that you can speak about anything and everything with your partner in total harmony.

What is intimacy for you, and how do you create that? Do you make a plan? Some people create a space and time where they can be truly intimate emotionally and physically with their partner. Some create a lovely bedroom space for this purpose—not just the bed, but maybe a couch or an open fire, with candles or wonderful music there or elsewhere in the home. So think about what you need in that area, to feel that your intimacy needs are being fulfilled.

The Masculine/Feminine Side

You've heard me talk a lot about beliefs that people have and about the realities that people live. It's very important to look at what you think a man needs in a woman, and what you think a woman needs in a man. Write these down. Recognize that these can be beliefs based on what you've seen in your environment from your friends, your parents, or other family. They can be based on your past experiences, which might not have been the most pleasant. They can be based on what globally, culturally, people believe. They may not be the truth.

After you write down what you think is most important for a woman to see and have in a man—and vice-versa—look at it and then go check if it's true. Check by maybe reading a book; or go online; or go to friends that are in wonderful relationships, and just ask them.

When I was single again in my mid forties, I finally decided to have a relationship. I wasn't kidding myself anymore—I truly wanted to be in one and admitted it to myself. I went to all my guy friends and asked them, "What do you think a man needs in a woman? What do you think a woman needs in a man?" I wrote down all their answers. When you do that with a lot of people, you reach a conclusion. This might be totally different from what you thought earlier, so look and broaden your vision. Go educate yourself! You might be surprised what you find out. I definitely did not anticipate what they shared with me. I never before looked at how men perceive things differently. For instance, men want their partner to be happy and take responsibility for everything. So when you are happy, they think they did it and when you are not happy it is also their responsibility!

How Do You Feel Loved?

Write down what you need in order to feel loved. What needs to be in place before you can feel it or believe it? Remember the example of the new husband and wife, the bills, and the flowers—what do *you* need to be loved? There are some people that love to hear their partner tell them how much they love them. I'm one of them. I can't get enough of it! I love to hear it. If he showers me with expensive gifts or expensive holidays, I totally like that too, but they don't necessarily make me feel loved.

My Alexander says he loves me on a more than daily basis. He surprises me with small things, like a chocolate or a flower or a card.

I have a girlfriend whose strategy for feeling loved is to receive a little love note every day from her husband. What is important for you to feel loved, so you can communicate it and get what you need.

Is it more important for you to hear it or feel it? Do you like and want hugs, kisses, caresses? Or do you want to be taken places, given gifts or surprises.

CHAPTER FIVE

Knowing Who You Are

Masculine versus Feminine: Yin and Yang

We all have a masculine side in us and we all have a feminine side. The trick is to find out what you are at your core, masculine or feminine. When you're masculine, you're probably more driven, more resolution-oriented. You like challenges. When you're feminine, you're often more creative, more in-the-flow, more in-the-present, nurturing.

Again, you have both masculine and feminine inside of you. But where do you feel happiest? Do you feel most happy when you're in your masculine energy or in your feminine energy?

For example, I'm feminine at my core, but I also have that masculine energy. I use my masculine energy as a tool when I'm on a project. When there's a deadline, I get things done in a very focused and fast way.

When I come with my masculine energy into my relationship—where there's already a masculine energy—then there are two masculine energies that collide and cause problems. That is the only time I have troubles in my relationship. When you have two males in a relationship, there will be fights, ego battles. Two females will irritate each other so much and will have catfights.

There is only room for one male and one female energy in a relationship. Where are you on the scale: 100% masculine or feminine, or in the middle, somewhat more masculine or more feminine?

In order to be happy in my relationship, I want to live where I feel happiest, and for me, that's at my feminine core. You have to look at where you are the happiest—in the feminine or in the masculine—and then decide on a partner with the opposite core.

Remember, opposites attract and create that chemistry. To have a lot in common as well insures the longevity of a relationship.

Masks

You might be feminine at your core, but you might wear a masculine mask. For example, in the business world, we currently have only one model of being successful: stepping into your masculine energy and being powerful in a masculine way.

If this matches your core, that's great. However, if you're feminine at heart, feminine at your core, but you live in that masculine energy, you may be very powerful and successful, but at the same time, you might not be happy and fulfilled. This is because you live in a different energy than who you are at heart and at your core. You can be powerful and successful in both ways, you know. Remember that you will always be the most powerful as yourself! It is the same the other way around, when you are masculine at your core, but you are wearing a feminine mask. Maybe because men have to be sensitive nowadays or you do not like confrontations, you do not know how to handle. You will not be happy either.

Find out who you are at your core, and then you can use the opposite energy as a strategy. It won't be something to live in, or something that comes by and just takes over—but a conscious choice.

When you are feminine at your core and you live that masculine energy, which you think it will give you power and success. But if you live totally in competition with the masculine energies at the office and at home as well, you will run into challenges, you will butt heads.

When you truly dare to step into your feminine power, then you discover that you can be as successful, as powerful in your own way.

It is the same when you dare to claim your masculine power people will relate to you, because you are real, authentic.

Beliefs

What do you believe about masculine power, about male power? What do you believe about feminine power? For a long time, I believed that being feminine meant being weak and insignificant. Being feminine meant being vulnerable. It meant you showed your weak side, your bad side. So there was no chance I would ever go to my feminine side. Some men believe that to be masculine is arrogant or overbearing or they think they would come across as too dominant.

When you live something you're not, people will sense that, and they will feel that something isn't quite right. They may not know what it is, but they will sense that there is incongruence, inauthenticity. They will sense that they'd better stay away from you because something doesn't click. They will not fully trust you and will not fully connect with you either.

Once I looked at my beliefs about feminine energy, I said, no wonder I'm not really feminine. I might have the appearance of being a total woman, but my energy definitely is towards the male side.

Once I changed my beliefs to "vulnerability is power," I changed all that. At first I thought I'd never ever want to be vulnerable. Being vulnerable means weak, and I am strong. But when I changed my belief, it became my power.

Through my vulnerability, I could step into that feminine power. And you know what? It brought me more success, more connections, and more friends than I ever would have dreamt of.

The same is true about male power. What is male power? Some people might find that when you step into that power, you might be aggressive or you might have a short fuse. But it's what you want to make of it.

When a true male-at-the-core steps into his power, he can also be gentle. I've met a lot of big tall men, and they refuse to step into their male power. They don't want to do that because, as they say, I'm big already. I have that male power, and people are scared of me. That is simply their belief.

When a man is centered, grounded, and stands straight and with ease, then he's totally in his male power. That is a lovely gift to all women. If men come across as aggressive, challenging, or in your face, it's because they make it that way. Power can actually be a rock of certainty, something to lean on. You make up yourself what you think femininity or masculinity are. What do you make them to be?

Where you feel the happiest is the place where you have to spend the most time. If you feel happiest and fulfilled when you're totally male, then that's your place. Spend as much time as you can in that place. If you love being in your feminine core, being feminine at heart; that's where you should spend most of your time.

Women have been saying for centuries that men have to be more sensitive. Now, finally, men *are* getting more sensitive, but now we call such a man feminine. And most women do not find this attractive.

There's a very interesting energy going on. Women are encouraged to be more masculine at their work, so they think it's a good thing. They get praise and results for it, so they have decided to live more in the masculine world. Men have been encouraged to be more sensitive and more romantic, so they lean towards being more on the feminine side. That might work in some areas.

When you look at the relationship area—that's *not* where it works. In the first place, both sexes are wearing masks, so you're not totally yourself. You're not living at your core, you're living together with masks, so it's very difficult to see what's what, who's who. It's very confusing. How do you react, how do you deal with such a thing?

When there is a challenge—maybe the woman comes out with a male energy, and the man's true masculinity flies out—then all of a sudden, you have a competition going on in the relationship.

You have a massive power struggle going on. There's two of a kind. There's no polarity and there's not enough difference, so there will be no passion. There will be grounds for a good friendship, but not for an intimate, loving, and passionate relationship.

The same happens when a man lives too much on his feminine side. When's he's masculine at his core, and all of a sudden you have two female energies in a relationship, it's a base for a good friendship. But when there are two female energies, there will never be a base for a great, wonderful, passionate and loving relationship.

Habits Bring Back Memories

We all have some years behind us. When you've lived for awhile on this planet, you have developed certain habits. Habits are great—nothing wrong with them—but you have to get awareness. When you live with a different mask than who you really are at your core, becomes a habit. And unaware of this you will bring this to your relationship as well. What you wear or what you have in your house may bring back memories. Sometimes they may bring you right back to a great memory, but sometimes they bring you back to a memory of a bad experience or painful past relationship. They may trigger some of the emotions linked to what happened way-back-when.

Pictures are great. Make sure the pictures you have in your house bring you back to great, loving moments. You might decide that pictures of former lovers or estranged friends may have to go.

Look at how you dress. What kind of clothes do you wear? What colors are they? What styles? What make-up do you use? What perfume do you wear? They can all bring you back to a memory, one that might be keeping you in the same place or doesn't serve you in some other way. Be in control—allow only good memories to come back.

For now, go into your closet and look at what clothes are hanging there. Are there colors or styles you might want to update? Go to a store where you try on some things you'd never ever wanted to before, and see if there's something new you can add to your closet.

Definitely give yourself a makeover. Go to a beautiful store and ask for a makeover. Use a different color for eye make-up or blush, and—most of all—change your perfume. We're all very olfactory, and there's a belief that you choose your partner with that sense, that sense of smell. Start a new updated you. Make yourself feel more confident. The same goes for men. Look at what you are wearing, change your aftershave, update your eyebrows and change your cologne.

Another thing you might make over is your peer group, your friends. We all have expectations. Guess what? Your friends all have expectations—about you.

Say that you want to have a relationship, and your peer group (your friends, your family) are totally used to your being alone. You're doing everything by yourself, your being the "strong one"—that's what they expect.

I'm not saying that you have to turn away from friends and family, but maybe it's time to update your group of friends. Maybe it's time to look for people who want to do something else, something new.

Maybe you need to have new group of friends, or add friends to your group that you can do different or special things with. Remember I told you earlier about a friend of mine who was only hanging out with her girlfriends? Later on, she got to know more people, and adding new friends was a wonderful thing. Through that, she eventually found her man.

Look at your peer group and ask, hey, who's supporting me? Is there anybody dragging me down? Are they a "neutral" or supportive group of people? The "neutral" people who say, "You're good just the way you are, don't change, you don't have to have a boyfriend or a girlfriend, you don't have to have a relationship, who cares?" —those are *not* the people you want to spend a lot of time with. They may in fact be dragging you down by comforting you.

Instead, spend time with people who spur you on, who say, "Come on, that's what you want--let's go and do something different, let's sign up for a course or a cruise or a theater subscription, so we meet new people." If you always do the same thing, you will always get the same results. If you want to change, do something different, maybe with different people!

There's one thing I'd like you to take on. Learn to walk with your invisible lover at your side. This is the secret to attracting the one you want to have in your life.

Do you remember a time when you were freshly in love? Maybe it was the first time you were ever in love. Do you remember how that felt, the butterflies in your stomach? How the world all of a sudden looked like a better place?

How everything seemed to be a success in your life? How whatever you were doing worked out? Some people say that when you're in love you see the world through rose-colored glasses, and that is probably true.

When you're in love, the world is great, everybody is kind, and luck is smiling upon you. It's all fantastic, and in that frame of mind, don't you feel terrific? I feel awesome when I'm in love. I feel great. I love it! Remember that when you're in that state, people are attracted to you and want to be in your presence. People want to come to you and hang out with you.

It's two-fold, this walking with your invisible lover. It makes you feel great *and* it attracts people to you. You train yourself to believe that your partner is already there. Your brain doesn't know the difference between fiction and reality, so if you can train your brain and yourself that your partner is already next to you, you walk with him or her.

If your love's next to you all the time, then you're starting something I call manifesting. You manifest that person already as being there, and that person only has to come and find you. This is the secret of getting your fulfilling relationship fast. Walk with your invisible lover at your side.

CHAPTER SIX

Getting Into a Relationship

Get Into the Game

You have to get into the game in order to be successful. If you're sitting at home waiting until your partner finds you, you might be in for a long sit.

One of the first things to do is to start dating. Get into the game! Your only objective is to have fun. You don't have to do anything else yet—just start dating and have fun. By dating, I mean just going out for a cup of coffee, a glass of wine, a cup of tea, or a walk on the beach. Keep it very simple and very light. The best would be if you could date three people at the same time.

Once you've been on a date, go home and evaluate that person against what you want and need in a relationship, and then make a decision. You say, yes, I want to see that person again, or no, that's it, he's not at all what I want, and you can let him go. Early in the dating game, you can make a choice whether that person fits your criteria or not.

Why do I say that you should date three people at the same time? This is because a lot of people date one person and they live in hope that this might be "the one." They want to give this person every chance, every benefit of the doubt. If you think you come from a model of scarcity, you think there aren't too many of "the ones" in this world. So if you have anybody even close, you think you have to do whatever it takes to keep him or her.

If you think you come from scarcity, then you won't have the courage to say no. If you know that there is an abundance of wonderful men and women in the world all waiting for you to meet them, you know that there's that special person out there who meets all your criteria and wants to be with you. When you know that there is this abundance, then you will have the guts and the courage to say, "I'll stick with my criteria. Don't be afraid to reject somebody early and move on. Dating three people at the same time makes this easier to do. It's easier if all your eggs are not in one basket at any given time.

Remember what you want and need—and if the person doesn't fit your main criteria or it's a total no, then it's easy to not go out with that person anymore. You're not involved! It's just one date—so it's easy to say, "You're great, but you're not what I'm looking for."

If you're in doubt, just go out with them again. Ask some more questions, and find out more about them. After that, reevaluate and decide. It's like a job interview, in a way. You have your job description, and you are responsible for deciding if it's a match.

Another thing: When you date three people at the same time, it gives you such a boost. It gives you the great feeling that you're desirable and totally attractive. You know they want you, so they're each giving you that self-esteem again, that confidence. And with that, you attract even more people.

In the dating game, you have to have an open mind. Sometimes we get caught up looking for a specific model of a person, and then we narrow everything down. In the beginning, it's just dating—remember, they're not "the one" yet. Be open to all kinds of experiences. And go out with somebody you might never have gone out with prior to doing this work.

I've gone out with guys who, at first sight, did not meet my criteria, but they were very nice and great company and we had a good night. At the end of the evening, I realized that I had been right and he wasn't the right person for a relationship. But so what? I had a great time, and some of those men have become good friends.

To be honest, I would never have married my husband if I had stuck with my closed-mindedness, saying to myself that "He has to look like this, and it has to be exactly like this." At first sight, my husband wasn't somebody I thought of as a relationship possibility. He was too young, he didn't live in the same country, he is from Germany and I live in The Netherlands ,he's an actor. I thought, "That's so far from who I am." So, at first, I thought it would never work out. But I stuck to my rule of having an open mind, and look at the result: I'm very happily married. He's the best thing that ever happened to me!

New Thoughts and Focus

We talked a lot in previous chapters about focus, especially about how easy it is to have a negative focus, and how negative thoughts have consequences for you. But at this point, you're beyond all that! Now it's time for you to develop some new thoughts and a new focus.

Decide what you want to newly focus on now. Do you want to focus on, "Yes, my partner is waiting for me. I just have to meet him," or are you still saying, "That person just has to come find me." So you are waiting and not taking action. Do you want to think of yourself as attractive, as being quite a catch, as being a prize? Do you want to think about yourself as beautiful and charming and bringing a lot to the table?

Now is the time for you to decide how you want to think about yourself, how you want to think about your relationships, the men and women in your life, the partner you want to attract into your life.

If you focus and think "It's possible," and if you have total trust and faith that it will happen—then it will happen. If you have the patience to stick to it and not say, "Okay, I've done it for two weeks—where's my partner?", if you have that inner faith and knowledge because your invisible lover is already at your side, if you know it will happen—*I promise you it will happen.*

It's so much fun to turn your thoughts and focus around. You immediately feel better when you focus on the positive. You feel better because you know that it will happen, it is possible. It's great to focus on having fun while meeting new people. Go out with new people— that's all you need to do for now.

As I said, I went out with a number of people. At first, after one date, it was, no, not really—nice guy, but not what I'm looking for. But with every guy I evaluated, I got the feeling that I was coming closer to what I needed. I said to myself, yes, I'm getting closer to my ideal. And when you see that progress in your dating, you also acquire the patience to wait until the one that's meant for you shows up. The last guy I dated before I met my husband was almost everything I wanted, but that's the trick: do NOT settle for less than you deserve.

I had a list. And we'll go over all the qualities and characteristics of your desired partner. We already went through a lot of the list in Chapter 4, "What Do You Really Want and Need in a Relationship?" It's not that I had written down 100 things and had to have all

100 on my list. There are different priorities. Some you absolutely need to have and others are negotiable, not so important.

But you do need to evaluate your dates, determine if you want to go out again, and recognize your progress in this area. Certainly, make sure you remember that you decided to be happy no matter what! But also make sure you bear in mind that you're looking for the relationship that will become and remain the most important in your life.

Remember, finding a relationship may not always be your first priority, but the more priority you give it, the sooner you will meet that wonderful person who's meant for you.

Set Your Boundaries

Take a good look at your boundaries. We all have boundaries, but often don't know where they are. You only determine where they are when somebody is trespassing, when somebody is violating them. Then, all of a sudden, you realize that you had some boundaries and some rules. It's better if you write them down up front so you know what they are and you can communicate them. It is important in dating to know how to communicate your boundaries as well.

When you are in a relationship already it is equally important to know each others boundaries so you can buid a healthy, stable and thriving partnership.

Look at what's okay and not okay for you in various areas. Now is the time to look at your boundaries, before you run into trouble with somebody who unknowingly steps over them! The best time to repair your roof is when the sun is shining (German proverb).

What boundaries do you have in the financial area? How far do you go? Let me explain. I know several women—and I was one—who spend nearly every penny on their partners. Is that okay? No, of course it's not okay. You have to make sure that financially, you do what's good for you. Spoil your partner occasionally, sure—but set your boundaries. Make sure that you live within your own budget and adjust your spending pattern. There are many other money issues where boundaries may have to be set, co-mingling of funds with partner, joint bank accounts, joint credit cards, joint property ownership, financial decision-making.

Look at your sexual boundaries. There are people with many limits, a few limits, or virtually no limits in this area. I think that most people definitely have a set of boundaries, whether they realize it or not. I definitely have a set of boundaries. Within these limits, I'm as happy and free as a bird. I know what I like and what I don't like, and I'm able to communicate this. My husband and I discuss everything, but before we try something new, we both have to feel comfortable with it

What are your boundaries regarding family and friends? Are you a person whose front door is always open? Can people just walk in and come into your home. Would you be comfortable if your in-laws came over unannounced? What other boundaries would you have with them visiting—perhaps for extended periods--or making unsolicited suggestions? Determine what you'd want with them, other family members, and friends.

What about your respective friends? What group of friends is your partner bringing with him or her?

"Where do you take your vacations?

When you have children in the house, set your boundaries. Put a lock on your bedroom door. Make sure the children know when's it's mommy-and-daddy time, and that they are not always first. The children have to know that mommy and daddy need to spend time with each other too, need to go out together. The sooner you teach that to your children, the happier and healthier they grow up— and with the right values for their own relationship.

In my earlier marriage, I was a total wimp. I didn't dare communicate what I wanted. And that may have had everything to do with the fact that I didn't feel deserving. I thought I would be seen as too demanding and selfish by my partner.

Now I totally know that I deserve the best. I deserve the most wonderful relationship on earth. I found the courage and the guts to gently and politely have a conversation about what was important for me.

Don't start a conversation by saying, "I demand that I have at least. . . ." You should never do that. You sit down somewhere nice together, you bring your notebook, you bring your wish list, you bring your boundaries, you bring all your thoughts about your relationship—and then you set up the rules of the game. Doing it this way serves you both.

It's like negotiating a contract. Go for what's most important to you, what's number-one on your list. Say, "You know what, this is important for me. This would make me feel absolutely loved and adored."

Always talk about your feelings. When you talk about how it makes you feel when your partner loves you, there is no problem at all. He will be willing to make you happy—he will want to make you happy. Then you'll listen to your partner and you'll figure it out together. Make it a win-win negotiation.

You should say, "I got my number one—what's yours?" You go down your partner's list and, in the process, you have fun creating that wonderful relationship. You're not just hoping that the relationship will work out miraculously. You're creating it, first on paper, and then in reality. You take turns so that you both feel supported. You both have a say in everything, and you both decide how your particular relationship will be uniquely wonderful.

What Actions Are You Taking?

Consider every action you can to get the relationship you want. Look at the things you've been doing, things that might not have led to the results you want. Remember, to have different results, take different actions. Check out things you haven't yet done.

I have this dear friend. She has just turned 60, and she wants to have a new relationship. I cheer her on, good for her! She said, "I'm very confident that I will meet him—and I will meet him in the next three months." I replied, "Yes, you're a beautiful woman, why not?" She then said, "But you know what? Although I know that's going to happen, I'm also going to check out all kinds of other things." She went to a very exclusive dating service, got a psychological report, and took it from there. She tells me, "It's fun! I have the feeling I'm doing something towards creating my new partner, finding my new partner."

Check out the Internet. There are hundreds, if not thousands, of Internet dating sites. Sometimes churches have dating sites. I know for sure that John Gray, author of the *Mars* and *Venus* books, has a dating site too. There are dating sites where you just "commit" to have lunch with each other, so you're not stuck for too long or for a big tab! This is a fabulous way of meeting lots of new people.

Make an action plan. Go do what you really like to do, and you will meet other people. Schedule the dates in your diary. For example, say to yourself, "Okay, I'm going to have one date a week.

Journal—get a little booklet and keep it by your side. Keep it on your nightstand, and every time you have an idea, scribble it down and later add it to the schedule in your diary.

Go and ask whatever loving couples you know—in your family, your circle of friends, and in your business— "What's your secret?" What do you do? How come you guys are so great together? What's the one thing that makes your relationship so great." Ask away!

Make sure you smile at everyone you meet—your neighbor, the store cashier, the person in the traffic jam with you—everybody. Smiling will give you a lot of unexpected contacts and surprises in life.

Last but certainly not least, check out the functions in your area. There is always plenty to do everywhere. See what's going on and go there! Go to dinners and seminars, take courses, go to museums or art galleries, do some volunteer work, hook up with a charity. There are all kinds of missions groups, charity work. Go and do whatever you truly like to do, and you will meet other people.

Chapter Seven

Recipe for Finding Your Love

Here is a list of everything you can do to prepare yourself. It's a step-by-step format that is very easy to follow.

Give yourself some time, and just go for it. Everyone who has followed this format has had major results in finding the right relationship.

--Describe who you are and who you want to be. There will probably be a difference!

--Get rid of all the thoughts, sayings, and ideas that you do not like. Here's how: Write them down, and next to each one, write the opposite, a positive version. Then say the negative ones in a real silly way—like Mickey Mouse or Speedy Gonzalez, with a different accent, or snort like a pig. You really have to go for it here! Do it together with a friend. Once you start laughing at the silliness, the old is gone. Now say your new beliefs with confidence and conviction over and over again for 28 days.

It is being proven that when you repeat anything consistently for 28 days it gets inside of you, it will become a habit, your truth.

Years ago I decided that I wanted to be a wise woman. I used the same technic and nowadys people comment on how wise I am!

--Create your ideal partner on paper. Ask yourself what you need and want in all areas of your life. Remember, you can and have to be totally selfish in this stage. Go for it—it's so much fun! Describe in detail how you want to partner to be in the following areas:

- romantically
- physically
- emotionally
- in the relationship
- sexually
- financially
- career-wise
- spiritually
- manners
- what is most important in life (values)
- hobbies
- how you will love each other
- how you will show up together [not clear what this means]
- how your partner will present you to the world

- how you like to be treated
- how you like to be talked about
- what your partner has to love and adore about you
- how you will know if it is "the one"
- special moments to experience

Good job ! Congratulations—you did it!

Now write all of it in the past tense, and read it every night. This is the power of *manifesting*. When you write in the past tense, your brain accepts it as the truth. It cannot distinguish what's real and what is not.

So—you will act as if these are already there, already manifested in your life.

- Decide to be happy and fulfilled, no matter what
- Live life as if your partner is already there, your invisible love
- Practice the feeling of being in love daily, start practising your flirting skills.
- Be willing to make your relationship the most important thing in your life (remember, importance is not the same as always giving it the highest priority)
- Change your color scheme, make-up, hair, perfume
- Start dating at least three people at the same time
- Evaluate after each date—check your list
- Have fun
- Have total faith that you will meet your partner
- Make a plan
- Do whatever it takes!

CHAPTER EIGHT

The Art of Flirting

What Is Flirting?

In the truest sense of the word, flirting just means banter, joking, repartee, wit, and chitchat. Flirting makes you and others feel happy. Flirting means having a good time with each other and having fun. Flirting usually is "cute." To me, flirting should be innocent: it should make all parties feel good!

Start flirting with yourself and with life, and then flirt with other people. (I'm going to explain what I mean in a minute.) Be happy about yourself and life, and you will be happy and giving towards others. *Bringing happiness to people*—actually that would be my very best definition of the word flirting. Flirting is another way to bring sunshine to other people. And when you're your happy self, it's easy to tease and be joyful, to joke and to have friendly happy conversations with others.

There is always something truly beautiful in everybody. Flirt with people and bring out their beauty—and your own.

Having a Flirtatious Attitude

Being flirtatious can be a way of living, a way of being. Being flirtatious means giving compliments to people, true heartfelt compliments—because everybody is beautiful. Someone has perhaps the most wonderful hair you've ever seen, or the most beautiful eyes, or has the most likeable demeanor. If you're truly looking, you can easily give sincere compliments!

Take yourself and others lightly. Joke about things, in the good sense of the word—keep it fun. There is a fine line between being funny and being sarcastic.

Did you ever hear the reasons why angels fly? Angels fly because they take themselves lightly. So from now on, be an angel--don't take life too seriously. Be an angel of flirting.

Flirting is also being happy, open, and honest. Be playful and remember—your own dating objective is having fun. If you're open, honest, and playful, you definitely will have a good time. When there's a lot of bantering, joking, and chitchat, you will at the very least strike up a great connection and have a beautiful time with others. That's what is actually most important.

People come into your life for a reason. Sometimes they come for a very short time, and sometimes they stay a little bit longer. Sometimes they stay forever. But you never know. Your objective should be to have a great time, whether it's for a lunch or cup of tea, several years, or your whole life.

We all have a gift to bring to others. We have a gift to bring to ourselves. By flirting, the gift you give to them and to yourself is a good time. The attention you give to them means you will also be in the present time with them, fully there—a gift to each of you.

Most people live either in the past or the future. They frequently carry every experience from the past with them in the present (usually the bad ones). They compare their new date with their old ones. They confuse old behaviors with new ones. They expect the same experiences. Beware of people who can only talk about their old relationships. They cling to them and hold on to them for dear life. Here's my advice to you: run!

People who live in the future always worry about what might happen. They are afraid of what is not even a reality, and in most cases will never be one.

We all have only the moment we are living in. Capture it, savor it. *Carpe diem*, "seize the day", seize your moment! Live, laugh, dance, sing. Give yourself and others the gift of enjoying the present, of being with each other fully.

Most people love to be the center of attention, right? If you're "there," giving them your time and your attention, and you're totally present with them, then you give them a precious gift.

When you read a book you don't like, you'll never read it again. So why lug around your whole past, including all the bad things? Why would you still carry it around with you?

A moment is just a moment. It goes by so quickly. So enjoy it--have fun! Give the people you're in contact with your presence, your being in the moment. Be attentive to them.

Start Being Flirtatious

First, look around you—look at your circle of friends and acquaintances and see if you know somebody who is great at flirting. By flirting, I mean someone who has that lightness, joyful playfulness. Or maybe there's a public figure or a film star that you know responds very well to people. These people communicate well to others, and there's always humor or laughter when they're around.

If you don't have that by nature, you can start learning it! Find somebody to be an absolute model for yourself, and start copying what they do. I've given you several approaches, but you have to figure out your own meaning of flirting, and choosing a model you like will go a long way. I recommend that you make others feel good. Make them have fun and laugh —and do so yourself. Create a personal plan and live it and learn it! When you flirt, life is fun. When you flirt, other people feel great and so do you.

We spoke about boundaries a couple of chapters ago, and there are boundaries in flirting. For me, flirting isn't sexual. It's not about being seductive or sensual. Save that for romantic situations. Flirting for me is more about having a good time with another person.

You also have to be aware of when flirting is appropriate and when it's time to be a little more serious. When you tune in to people, when you use all your senses to get information about where they are, then you will know whether the time is right to play full-out, to release that inner flirt—or whether it's time to be more serious. Adopting flirting as a way of life I think would be a very good thing!

CHAPTER NINE

The Stages of a Relationship

Stage 1 Desire a realationship
Stage 2 Dating
Stage 3 Being in love
Stage 4 Mutual love
Stage 5 Fulfilling love
Stage 6 Unconditional love

Stage 1: Desire a Relationship

The first stage of a relationship is wanting one! By now, you probably know whether you want one right now or not. You need to desire that relationship. It's not something you shrug your shoulders over and go, "Oh well—it would be great if I had one, and it would be okay if I didn't have one." I have a friend who always says she wants a partner, but everything else in her life always seems more important. As we have seen, what you focus on is what you create in your life. Where focus goes, energy flows.

It's important to know that in order to get that person you want by your side, you need to desire it, you really need to want it. You need to crave it. You need to say things like, "I would love having a relationship. I would love being in a relationship. I want to have a relationship. That relationship would be good for me. I crave that relationship. So build up this desire.

This is the first step towards getting that relationship. Say, "I am ready. I want to have a relationship as soon as possible. I want to have the right one for me. I want a relationship where I can express myself fully, where I can give and share freely, where I can receive and have mutual unconditional love, respect and acceptance."

Stage 2: Dating

We talked about dating. Remember, have fun, date three people at the same time. Do whatever it takes to get dates, and get in the game. Date people even if you "know" that it might not work out. What the heck—you have to practice your dating skills, right? If you don't practice your skills, you may never the person you're meant to be with. Broaden your vision, broaden your horizon, and start dating.

Start dating all the women you meet, all the men you meet. I'm exaggerating here, of course, but you get the message. You need to get into this game, and that means going out onto the field. In many ways, it's a numbers game. Sitting at home will *not* get you your partner. Live in abundance and date several people. At this stage, you are exploring and having fun. Do not limit yourself by judging people up front, by "deciding" that they are too short, too tall, too thin, too young or too old. Have an open mind and you might discover that your frog is a prince or princess after all.

Remember, a single date should last only a short period of time. If you don't like the person, you're not stuck with them for hours and hours. Have a cup of tea or a glass of wine: your only objective is to have fun. But be curious about them. Be curious about what kind of person you have in front of you. Go ahead and ask them all kinds of questions, so you get to know them.

Be interested in that person. Be truly interested in what they're about, what kind of work they do, and what their interests are. By asking questions, you find out soon enough if this is someone you want to go out with again. Be playful, be fun—but also be curious and genuinely interested.

Stage 3: Being in Love

Here, you have those butterflies in your stomach. You know that you're majorly attracted to that person. In this stage, you're not dating three people anymore. You've decided this is the person who meets most or enough of the criteria on your list and the one you feel totally attracted to.

You are in love. You experience the beauty of being in love and know that life is good. Everything is beautiful. You feel beautiful and sexy too. You also feel powerful—you do things easily and quickly, and whatever you do will be successful. It's a wonderful stage in your life!

My only advice to you is to enjoy this period totally. Enjoy it to the utmost. When you're both totally in love, this is the foundation of what can be the most wonderful relationship in your life.

You're still curious, and you're still find out more about your potential partner. You're still learning about their life, their family and their friends. Now would be a good stage to really explore their connections and feelings about their family and friends. Is their family still alive? Do they love their mom and dad? What kind of friends do they have? Keep an eye on your boundaries, though. Especially at the beginning of a relationship, many people tend to be too flexible, too forgiving, because they want to please the other. *Remind yourself that you still have to decide if you are in this for the long haul.* For example, if the person you love has a horrible relationship with their parents, it's best to check out very carefully from which side the tension or problem is coming. Likewise, if he or she has no friends, you'd better check out why not.

It's still being in love if you're getting to know each other and checking up on things! And hopefully, getting to know each other will make your love even stronger and the experience becomes more fantastic. Totally enjoy those butterflies in your stomach!

Stage 4: Mutual Love

For me, there's a difference between being in love and having mutual love. Being in love is exciting. It's the excitement of it being new. It's the excitement of exploring each other in every area. Mutual love, on the other hand, means you know for sure that that person really loves you. Mutual love is saying: yes, I love you, you're the most important person in my life. I totally, deeply, and completely love you with all your weaknesses and strengths, and with everything that makes you special and unique. Mutual love means you can trust and respect that person.

This is the stage where you connect on a very deep level. This is the stage where you feel happy that you both love each other. This is the stage where you let the world know that you're a couple, an item--that you're totally exclusive and that you chosen each other. This is the stage where you start thinking that this may well be the person I've been looking for my whole life, the person whom I want to spend the rest of my life with.

Stage 5: Fulfilling Love

Fulfilling love is where you start putting the a structure in place. This is where you start talking about what you need in order to feel even more loved and supported. The word "need" here doesn't mean that you're "needy." This is because when you're happy and you create that happy life, you will get whatever makes you happy and fulfilled. It will be a relationship between two whole independent people who are capable of giving and receiving unconditionally. They have made a choice to be together not because they "need" the other to provide something they lack. It's abundance again. *This is where you lay the foundation for your forever love!*

It's the stage where you communicate with each other about what makes you feel totally loved and supported. You describe what your partner can do for you to make you feel loved and supported, and you also find out what you can do to make him or her totally happy. This is where you start exploring what things you can put in place to make sure that both you and your partner are totally happy. This is so critical. When you lay a strong foundation, it makes it so much easier later on. Get to know what makes your partner happy, and you too. It's simply asking the questions: what makes you really happy, what makes you feel really supported, what makes you feel really loved — what else?

Once you've done that, once you've put that structure in place, you won't even have to think about it anymore. You just put it in a schedule, or it becomes a habit, and you will do everything you can to make each other very happy. And don't forget about the importance of the little surprises and creating your magical moments! You have fulfillment in that love; that love is giving you everything. That love is giving you the base, the foundation, for creating an absolutely extraordinary life in every area.

When your foundation is solid, you will always be able to fall back on it. It's something that will catch you if something happens—it's your safety net. It's your own magic place that gives you deep fulfillment and will bond you very intimately. Deep fulfilling love will make you want to stay with this person forever.

Stage 6: Unconditional Love

We are all human and therefore fallible. We have great strengths and great weaknesses. That's how we are unique. Every one of us is different. It's meant to be that way. What would it be like if we were all the same? It would be pretty boring! Be happy that you're a unique person and understand that your partner is unique too.

When there is true unconditional love, you love each other, period. You cherish that love. You nourish that love. You keep that love in a very special, magical, beautiful golden box with a bow tied around it. You keep it safe. You will do everything to protect that love. Nobody else can touch that love—it's yours and your partner's. No matter who you are, what mood you're in, or what happens in life, that love is safe and that love is sacred. Cherish it, nurture it.

When you're unconditional in your love, you don't think, "If only my partner were more attentive, then I would love him even more." Whether he's attentive or not, you love him. When he's not attentive enough, you say, "You know, honey, I love you so much—and I will love you no matter what – but what would make me feel even happier would be if every morning, we had five minutes, maybe at breakfast, for you to give me a little kiss and a little hug."

Whatever's going on in life or between you and your partner, you will work it out. You will sit down together and work out all challenges and put satisfying solutions in place, knowing that your love will always remain untouched. You will come up with whatever solution you need to overcome that hurdle. Your love is eternal and unconditional.

Chapter Ten

Rules of a Relationship

Never Take Things Personally

One of the rules of having a great relationship is: Whatever happens, you should never take it personally. It's so easy to take it personally when something comes up. When you have a conflict, you feel it as an attack on you. You think it is all about you. And you know what? Most of the time it isn't. It has nothing to do with you. It's about your partner—how they take things, how they feel about what's happening, what meaning they give to it. The best you can do is control your emotions, and just love, reassure, and support your partner.

When women are upset, they have to vent; they have to get it out. It's never about the lover in the relationship—it's all about the woman. They use the relationship as a vehicle to vent about whatever is going on. Masculine energy usually withdraws and becomes silent and non-communicative.

Women may rage as if they're being personally attacked, as if the issue is all about them, but their mates need to understand that the true situation may actually have nothing to do with them personally.

Men sometimes need to blow off steam. A man does that in a relationship—that's what relationships are for as well. As a woman, don't take it personally—it's not about you. It's about them blowing off steam. It's all about how we cope with challenges and problems. Do not take their problem on—leave it with them.

I have friends who have been married for a long time. When I asked them their secret, he said, "I'll love my wife forever because when I'm in an angry mood or not in the mood to do anything, or I don't want anything, she recognizes it for what it is. It's just a stage. She blows me off. She goes and does something that makes her happy and leaves me be. Eventually, I come around and we return to the normal, wonderful relationship we have."

Never Take Things Out of Context

You have to make sure that whenever you talk about something, it stays in that context. When you take words out of their original frame of reference, they get lives of their own, and that's a very dangerous thing. When you only remember snippets of conversations, they can acquire a totally different meaning. So when you look at a challenge, always look at the context in which the resulting words were used, and remember to keep them limited to that challenge. Never ever take them out of that context.

Remember when you were a child and you played a game where you had to pass on a message? After it had been passed on ten times, the message did not even remotely resemble what had been said in the first place. People are really good at deleting and otherwise distorting conversations. Be clear what you say and in repeating what you hear.

Never Question Your Partner's Intent

We talked about unconditional love in the last chapter. When you have that unconditional love, you know that your partner's intent is always good.

But we humans are limited. Sometimes you want to say something, but then it comes out all wrong. Did that ever happen to you? It often happens to me. When you're together and when you have that great love, then you need to know that your partner's intent is always good. It's never about their intent. When you know that they mean well, then it's easier to hear what's really going on, and it's easier to make things right.

If you question their intent, you're actually questioning the love your partner has for you. You're questioning the love you have for them. But when you keep your love sacred, when you keep it out of the argument, you know that it's never meant to be any other way. The only thing you need to do is clear things up and put a solution in place.

Be Committed to Your Relationship

Again, your relationship has to be the most important one in your life. If there's something going on, then you need to be there for your lover, your partner, your wife or your husband.

When you're committed to your relationship, if you're traveling or otherwise by yourself and you see somebody who's attractive or nice, you can smile or wave—but you know that you would never do anything to harm or jeopardize your relationship.

When you've chosen your love—when you're in that fulfilling, mutual unconditional love—you're committed. You're committed to do whatever it takes to make that relationship the best ever and to keep it very, very special.

Work Out Your Challenges

We all have challenges—that's life. If there were no challenges in life, it would be boring. The only people without challenges are dead people. You *will* have challenges and you can work them out.

Whenever something is going on, make a note of it. Then pick a specific time to make a plan for your challenge. There can be challenges on all levels. There can be challenges with finances, with moving house, with work, with kids and other family, and with friends. When things get difficult, people may start questioning their own love or their partner's. They start doubting. Well, I advise you not to doubt. Your mutual love is there—keep it alive.

Remember, to keep that love safe, sit down together just the two of you and create a plan to work out your challenges, knowing that your love is always there. That's a given, that's the base, that's solid. From that place, you can work out anything.

Address Each Other in a Special Loving Way

Often, at the beginning stages of a relationship, you will address each other in very special ways. You will have loving nicknames for each other. You call each other "my love," "my pumpkin," "my adored one," whatever you come up with. But then, in a later stage, you forget to do that. You forget to be special to each other because you take each other for granted. When someone or something becomes too familiar, we typically can no longer see their beauty, their uniqueness, their wonder, their magic. We see them as normal. You forget to be grateful for what is in your life because it has been there for awhile. Please do yourself a favor. Every day, take a look at yourself, your partner, and your love with fresh new eyes, as if it were the very first time again.

Go and say to yourself, "I've found a partner. I have this great love-mission accomplished." Remind yourself how special it is, how wonderful it is that you have each other. That's something you need to practice daily. Be grateful for the wonderful love you share and the wonderful partner, lover, husband or wife you have in your life.

It's special, it's a gift—so in order to honor that extraordinary present, address each other in that special, loving way. You can even ask your partner, how would you like me to address you? What would you most like for me to call you? Make sure you make that a habit. Make sure to do that for each other every day and everywhere.

Believe in Yourself and in Your Love

Believe in your partner. Believe in your love. I often notice that this is true of couples in the beginning stages of their relationship, but they forget about it later on.

My husband is from Germany. In Germany, they have a saying that after six months of marriage or other relationship, you go back to "normal" day-to-day life. The fun is over, the butterflies are gone; that's it. It's a universal belief there, but you don't have to believe it. Make up your own beliefs! It's like saying, okay, we can have all this magic for six months, and now it's over. You can make sure you keep that love growing all the time. We were well aware of this belief, because people told us all the time. So we made a commitment to each other to keep our love alive, take time to love and be with each other. Be grateful and thankful every day that we have this amazing love in our lives.

When you believe that you can have magical love, you can create it and keep it in your life. You know how to do it. First of all, believe in yourselves. When you know that your partner also shares this belief, that love is possible, that love is a there for us as a gift from God, from the Universe, it's there to make our lives wonderful, no matter what the circumstances.

Always believe in that love. It is there. It is possible. You just have to believe in it. It's like the story of Peter Pan and Wendy. If you believe you can fly, you can fly. Fly in your relationship, and shoot for the moon. If you miss, you are still in the stars! If you believe you can love and get love in return, you will have it.

Be Passionate

According to many people, passion is also time-related. Of course there is passion when you're first in love. Then, when your relationship becomes steadier, when you know each other a bit longer, they say passion isn't so important. Or it may disappear. People give themselves an excuse for not being passionate anymore.

Passion comes from remembering who you are. Passion comes from remembering who your partner is. Passion becomes a state of mind. It's creating that time when you can express that incredible love to each other—and by the way, that's not always in the bedroom. It's in the emotions you feel for each other, and the time you spend together and create for each other. It's in how you talk about each other and how you surprise each other. Passion is in believing that you have this magical love.

Passion Is a Way of Living.

Have you ever met people who are passionate about their mission in life, passionate about what they're doing, whether it's a career, sports, or helping people? Do you know what it's like to be in the presence of such a person? We have icons that we all recognize were passionate—like the famous Martin Luther King, Jr., President Kennedy, Mother Theresa.

It's a gift and we all have it. You only have to choose whether you want to use it or whether you want to ignore it and forget it. Make it a part of your life. Be passionate about yourself, your partner and your love, your life. Make daily reminders that passion is a must. It's exciting and it makes you feel alive.

Be Spontaneous

Be spontaneous! Do fun stuff. Surprise people—and certainly surprise your partner. Make a list of all the things you would love to have or do, or the places you would love to go. Make a list for yourself, and another. Then when you're in the mood to do something spontaneous, you can go to the list and pick one that you or your partner will like.

Do fun stuff and don't get into a rut. Don't get into a habit of always doing the same things at the same time on the same day; at some point, you'll be bored to death. Make sure there's spontaneity to keep your relationship alive. Have the guts to call your partner up in the middle of a work day and ask, "Do you have something urgent to do? No? Then come on, we'll catch a plane and fly to Paris, go to lunch at the Ritz!" Or come home with a big bunch of flowers. Do the unexpected things that will make your relationship feel alive and juicy!

No Egos In the Relationship

When you need to feel significant, remember that significance is tied to having an ego. And, as we learned in Chapter 1, egos have no place in a relationship. When you need to feel significant, remember that you're the chosen one. You have been chosen by your fantastic partner. Remember that you have that wonderful love. Remember that you're one of the happy few with such a great gift. It's that love that should and will make you feel significant

If there is an ego struggle, a power struggle, or some other kind of fight for significance in your relationship, ask yourself these questions: Is this worth it? Is the feeling of being significant more important than the feeling of being loved? What do I value more—significance or love?

If you have the need to be the best, to earn the most, to have control over everything in your relationship, then ask yourself: what's missing? What makes you crave these things instead of giving and receiving love? Why do you need to compete with your lover?

Make sure you get your significance in a healthier way by remembering that you already are!

Support Each Other's Dreams

We all have dreams. We all have something in our lives that is special for us. It might not be *your* dream, it might not be what *you* want to do, but support your partner in achieving their dream. It can be something small or big—but make sure that you support him or her.

I remember a friend who was married with three kids. He was in a great relationship. He had this dream of climbing Mt. Kilimanjaro. He kept postponing it because of his business, his children, you name it. He had all kinds of excuses for himself not to go for it.

His wife knew his wish. She made up an excuse for a party and we were invited. When we were all there, she brought in a cake she had baked in the form of Mt. Kilimanjaro, and next to the cake was a ticket for his flight to Africa to start his trip.

I was so touched by that. That's truly supporting each other's dreams. So go for it—find out what the dream is and support your partner every way you can.

Convert Expectations to Standards

Most people have expectations. I challenge you to convert expectations into standards. Expectations are not normally communicated. And if you expect something from another person, your lover, your partner, without having clarified what it is—that's unfair. How could they possibly know? Can they mind-read and be correct, and magically know what you want?

You can never expect something from anybody without specifically communicating what it is. In a relationship, expectations can be deadly because you will be disappointed when your partner cannot read your mind. They can't know by looking at you what's going on, nor what you need them to do to make you feel loved or happy again.

Create a set of standards. These are like your marriage vows, or, if you're living together, a sort of love contract where you say:

- I promise to always love you.
- I promise to express my love in the morning and in the evening by saying or by doing. Set your standard.
- I promise whenever there's an argument we never go to sleep without having a solution.
- I promise that you may come up to me at any time and ask me for a solution for any problem
- I promise that I will always be present when you need my time. I promise to listen to you.

Make a list of your standards, what your code of conduct will be in your relationship. Sign it, hang it on the wall, and live by it.

CHAPTER ELEVEN

How to Avoid and Resolve Conflicts

Communicate Your Upset

We all live by rules. Societies are run by rules, and that's a good thing. You pick up rules from your parents, your school, your friends, from traffic signs!

You might not be aware of some of "your" rules. And it might be your rules that upset you — the same situation might never upset another person. For instance, when somebody is talking to me in a very loud voice and is very close to me, I usually get a little upset because one of my rules is that this is a sign of anger. And another of my rules is that you are never supposed to show that you are angry with others; you communicate your upsets and work it out. Someone else that's being spoken to in the same way might not mind at all. If you get upset, you need to communicate that.

Then, if something else happens, you stack it on top. You continue stacking things and then suddenly you can't keep yourself in rein anymore, and it all comes out—and in an ugly way.

Whenever something upsets you, it needs to be communicated. However small it is, you need to do that and do it in a very special way.

One of the ways I learned from Cloe Madanes is to carry a little notebook in which you write down your upsets, and you have a scheduled meeting with your partner in a public place. If you're not good at arguments, it's better to do it in a public place. It's like you're having a board meeting with the other executive in your marriage or relationship.

During that meeting, you have to promise yourself to just listen. Listen to what's going on without defending yourself. Defending ourselves is one of the first things we do when we hear there's an upset. Instead, listen to what's going on, *then* talk about things, how to avoid it the next time, and how to put a solution in place.

But remember, when you talk about your upsets, talk about what you felt, your feelings. Don't go pointing fingers and saying, "What you did was wrong." No, you talk about your own feelings. You say things like, "You know, honey, when this and that happened, it made me feel hurt, it made me feel sad, and I know that's not you. I know that's not your intention because I know you love me. But I need you to know how it made me feel."

"Honey, the next time, can you please do it a little differently? Can you please do it in a different way?" And then you end with, "Okay, would that work for you too?" That's how you communicate your upsets. You put a strategy in place so you can avoid misunderstandings the next time.

Take Time For Each Other

Spend time together. My husband and I are very busy, and we're both passionate about the work we do. We do very different things, very opposite things, but we're both passionate about our careers. And when we've both been extremely busy and haven't taken the time to connect, chances are that there will be an argument bigger than if we had been truly connecting.

Although we can be very busy, we've learned to always take the time to at least call each other. We always take the time to be with each other. So schedule time when you can be with each other without distractions and without children. In my opinion, children can be the biggest distraction in a marriage. When you have children, it's of the utmost importance that you schedule time for just the two of you. Schedule that daily and also as part of the weekend—time just for the two of you. It's very important to stay connected and have time for true intimacy.

The third strategy is to really understand what makes your partner feel loved and supported. Write it down, make a whole checklist, and know what you can instantly do to make your partner feel loved. Know what you can do when they're not in a good mood. Do you need to leave them alone? Can you do something funny or playful to get them out of that mood? What can you do?

My husband likes to be left alone if something is not going right. Then, half an hour later, everything is okay again, and we can speak about it. I know that whatever is going on, it's not about me. It's his thing and he has to work it out. When that's over and done with, we can talk about everything.

Another example: we had something we needed to work out between the two of us, nothing major, just a little thing. He was in Germany, and I was in America. He wanted to resolve it like a "true man"— over the phone, immediately. At that moment, I said, "You know, honey, I feel very alone at this moment. I miss you so much. I haven't seen you in a week. Can we please wait until we're together, until we feel that connection again, until we're in each other's arms, and I've seen you? Then I promise we'll pick a time and then we'll work it out." And his answer was: "of course my love that would make it easier for us and feel a lot better too".

Don't Settle for Connection Over Love

Maybe you've heard people say that in order to have a great relationship, you have to work hard at it. You can focus on the fact that it's hard work, or you can say everything in life needs to grow. If you look at your garden, it grows or it dies. When you have a beautiful love, then you need to grow that love. You need to care for it and nurture it. You need to devote some time to it and put some strategies in place. It's the same as having a health goal or a financial goal: you make a plan and follow through with actions.

Love is special and it's great to have it in your life. But in order to keep that love and to avoid conflicts, you need to put a plan in place on how to grow and to maintain it.

Sometimes it's easier to settle for less. If you settle for just connection, friendship, or just plain having somebody around, then chances are that you're having a lot of conflicts. If you're not happy, your partner isn't happy. It's not how you started out with each other, and it's just a breeding ground for challenges. Make sure then when you have love, you keep on growing and nurturing it. Otherwise you will lose it.

Take, for instance, children. When a woman has a child, it's such a beautiful, exhausting and time-consuming experience that it can appear to the father that the child is more important than he is. You need to sort this out and understand what's going on. You need to know what your partner needs in that moment to feel loved and important.

Take Responsibility For Your Actions

We spoke about intent in the previous chapter. It's almost never people's intention to hurt others. But when it happens, you have to take responsibility for your own actions, and you have to take responsibility for your words.

When you take responsibility, you stand up and say "You're right, that wasn't very nice of me to say," or "It wasn't very thoughtful of me to put it in that way, and I'm very sorry." Do that—and you not only make the other person feel better, you automatically feel better yourself.

Being responsible for what you do and say is important to avoid conflicts. When you take responsibility, you can then do something about the situation. If you assign the blame to others or to circumstances, then it will actually leave you in a state of helplessness, in a state where you no longer can do anything about it. And then the upset will keep on lingering because you think it is out of your control.

When you say, yes it was I who created it, I did that, I didn't think, I didn't have enough information and I take full responsibility for it, you have my sincerest apologies, I will do whatever I can to put another solution in place—then you can start working out challenges and problems.

Interrupt Your Patterns

You have to come up with a way to interrupt your own and each other's patterns. Again, sometimes we're in a good mood and sometimes not. When I'm in a bad mood, what I often do is take my egg timer and set it on a specific time. If there's something minor going on, I put my egg timer on ten minutes. When the alarm goes off, I promise myself that I'll change my mood. Meanwhile, I do whatever it takes to change my mood—dance, listen to music, read.

When there's something serious going on, then you can take a longer time. But that egg timer works for me as a reminder that, hey, I've been sulking enough, it's over now, do something else, time's up.

You can also do that for your partner. But before you do that, you have to make sure you discuss what specifically you're going to do to interrupt that bad mood! If you just come up with any old thing you think is funny but your partner doesn't, then you're in trouble.

Make sure you have a list of things you can do that makes your partner laugh, or that make your partner reach out to you and give you a big hug. It's fun to do that because nobody likes to be in a bad mood, right? Everybody likes to be happy, so if you can do that for your partner when they're not in the best of moods, if you can change their pattern—that is again such a gift, coming from the love in your relationship.

For instance, when my husband is in a bad mood (and he's almost never in one), I just start tickling him. He can't stand it, but he still likes it. Then we have a good laugh. We give each other a big hug and everything is good again. So make sure that you put some funny, loving pattern interrupts in place so you can help each other shift into a better mood—and be in one most of the time!

Chapter Twelve

Recipe for Growing and Maintaining Your Love

Well done, you read the whole book! I am proud of you. It shows me how committed you are to taking charge, to creating the relationship you deserve.

If you are already in a relationship, here's the recipe for growing and maintaining your love:

- Describe what is great in your relationship.
- Describe what initially attracted you to your partner, and associate yourself every day to the above.
- Look at what you want to change, or what is missing, and decide what YOU can do about it.
- Check your beliefs about yourself, your partner, and your relationship, and exchange the ones you don't like, or those which are not supporting you, for great ones.

- Communicate to your partner what your boundaries are, what you like and do not like, in a friendly and elegant way. Find out each other's rules.
- Communicate what you need in order to feel loved and supported.
- Let go of your old stories and excuses about past relationships.
- Take responsibility for your words, behavior, and actions
- Check in how you speak and think about your partner, and be each other's number-one fan.
- Practice flirting with each other.
- Start dating your partner again.
- Plan time together.
- Plan time to talk.
- Set up a rescue plan for emergencies.
- Learn how to support each other in upsets.
- Be present for each other.
- Plan and organize special wonderful dates.
- Be grateful for what you have.
- Associate with the positive and disassociate from the negative.
- Make a decision to be happy and fulfilled.
- Live in unconditional love.
- Practice daily the feeling of being in love.
- Be willing to make your relationship the most important in your life. But remember it is not always your first priority
- Love your children, but make your partner number one.

- Let go of ego and of the need to be more significant than your partner.
- Communicate your sexual needs, wants, and desires.
- Check out the "other person(s)" in your relationship.
- Have fun and together and laugh often.
- Make a plan for how you want to spend time and what you will you to grow and enhance your love for each other.
- Each night, tell your partner one thing you love them for.

Thank you for spending time with me. I wish you the most amazing loving relationship ever.

Dr. Connie Schottky-Osterholt

BUY A SHARE OF THE FUTURE IN YOUR COMMUNITY

These certificates make great holiday, graduation and birthday gifts that can be personalized with the recipient's name. The cost of one S.H.A.R.E. or one square foot is $54.17. The personalized certificate is suitable for framing and will state the number of shares purchased and the amount of each share, as well as the recipient's name. The home that you participate in "building" will last for many years and will continue to grow in value.

Here is a sample SHARE certificate:

HABITAT FOR HUMANITY

THIS CERTIFIES THAT

YOUR NAME HERE

HAS INVESTED IN A HOME FOR A DESERVING FAMILY

1985-2005

TWENTY YEARS OF BUILDING FUTURES IN OUR
COMMUNITY ONE HOME AT A TIME

1200 SQUARE FOOT HOUSE @ $65,000 = $54.17 PER SQUARE FOOT
This certificate represents a tax deductible donation. It has no cash value.

YES, I WOULD LIKE TO HELP!

I support the work that Habitat for Humanity does and I want to be part of the excitement! As a donor, I will receive periodic updates on your construction activities but, more importantly, I know my gift will help a family in our community realize the dream of homeownership. **I would like to SHARE in your efforts against substandard housing in my community!** *(Please print below)*

PLEASE SEND ME _____ SHARES at $54.17 EACH = $ $_____

In Honor Of: _____

Occasion: (Circle One)   HOLIDAY   BIRTHDAY   ANNIVERSARY

   OTHER: _____

Address of Recipient: _____

Gift From: _____ *Donor Address:* _____

Donor Email: _____

I AM ENCLOSING A CHECK FOR $ $_____ PAYABLE TO HABITAT FOR

HUMANITY OR PLEASE CHARGE MY VISA OR MASTERCARD *(CIRCLE ONE)*

Card Number _____ Expiration Date: _____

Name as it appears on Credit Card _____ Charge Amount $ _____

Signature _____

Billing Address _____

Telephone # Day _____ Eve _____

PLEASE NOTE: Your contribution is tax-deductible to the fullest extent allowed by law.
Habitat for Humanity • P.O. Box 1443 • Newport News, VA 23601 • 757-596-5553
www.HelpHabitatforHumanity.org

9 781600 376832